Ancient Persia

The Rise and Fall of the Persian Empire - From Cyrus the Great and Darius to Xerxes, Alexander the Great, and the Fall of Persepolis

Samuel Corwin

Table of Contents

Introduction
Why Ancient Persia Matters

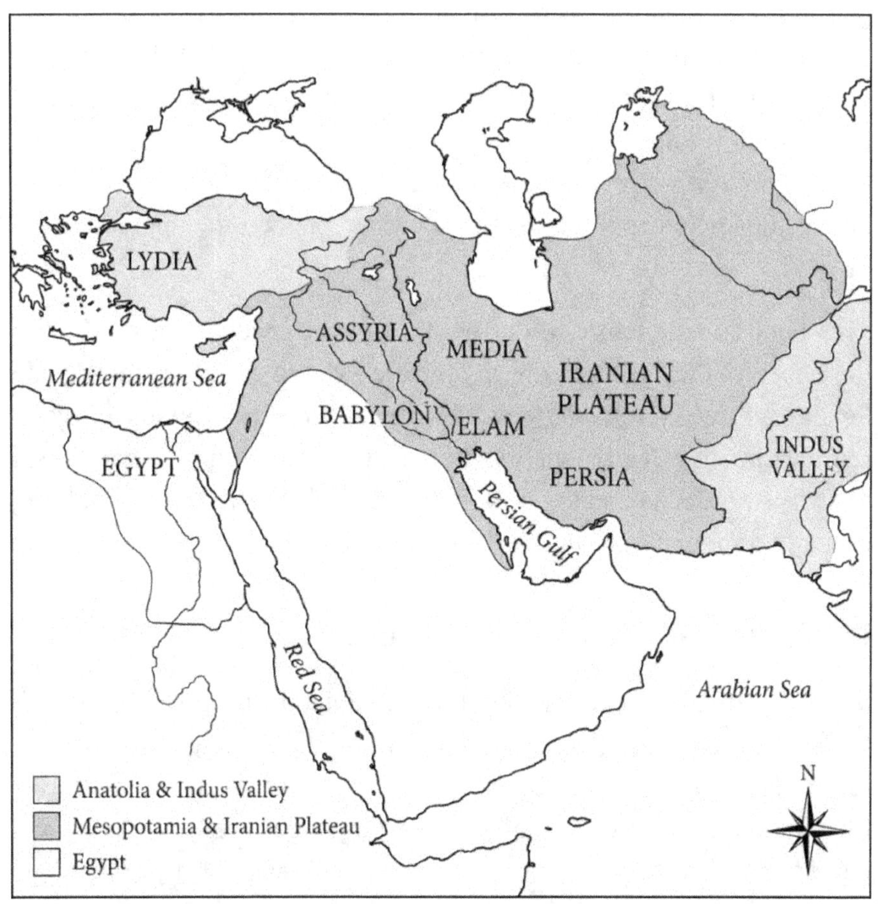

The Ancient Near East, 7th century BCE

Ask most people what they know about ancient Persia, and the same images surface: a vast, faceless army darkening the horizon at Thermopylae, a tyrannical king demanding earth and water as tokens of submission, a civilization defined almost entirely by its conflicts with Greece. That version of Persia is vivid, dramatic - and profoundly incomplete.

For too long, the story of one of history's greatest empires has been told by its enemies. The Greeks wrote brilliantly, and they wrote to win. Their accounts of Persia - filtered through Herodotus, shaped by the pride of city-states that had survived against impossible odds - gave us a civilization seen through the wrong end of the telescope. Persia appears distant, exotic, and ultimately defeated. What gets lost in that framing is something far more interesting: a civilization that governed millions of people across three continents, that pioneered ideas about religious tolerance and administrative efficiency centuries before those concepts had names, and that shaped the ancient world in ways we are still tracing today.

This book is an attempt to correct the angle of view. Not to dismiss the Greeks - their records are invaluable - but to read them alongside Persian sources, archaeological evidence, and the growing body of scholarship that has spent the last century recovering what Persia actually was. What emerges is not a villain's story. It is something richer and more surprising than that.

Persia Beyond the Greek Narrative

When Cyrus the Great founded the Achaemenid Empire in 550 BC, he did something that no ruler before him had managed on quite the same scale: he built a state designed to hold together an almost incomprehensible diversity of peoples, languages, and gods. Within a generation, the empire stretched from the Aegean coast to the edges of Central Asia. By the time of Darius I, it encompassed territories from Egypt to the Indus Valley - a landmass larger than any political entity the ancient world had yet seen.

At its peak, around 500 BC, the empire's population has been estimated at somewhere between 17 and 35 million people. That range tells you something important: we are still learning. But even the lower figure represents roughly half the world's population at the time living under a single administrative system. This was not a simple conquest state, a machine for extraction and tribute. It was a civilization that had to solve genuinely hard problems - how do you communicate across vast distances when dozens of languages are spoken? How do you govern peoples with radically different customs without provoking constant rebellion? How do you build roads, collect taxes, and administer justice across terrain that ranges from the Nile Delta to the Hindu Kush?

The Achaemenids found answers. Not perfect answers, and not without violence - no ancient empire was built gently - but answers that were sophisticated enough to influence every major empire that came after them.

Why Ancient Persia Is Misunderstood

Part of the problem is source material. The Persians left records - administrative tablets, royal inscriptions, the magnificent ruins of Persepolis - but they did not produce the kind of sustained historical narrative that the Greeks did. Herodotus wrote *The Histories*. No Persian Herodotus survives, if one ever existed. That asymmetry has consequences. When one side of a conflict writes the history and the other side does not, the story tilts.

What the Greek sources give us is a Persia defined by its relationship to Greece: the invasions under Darius I, the famous campaigns of Xerxes I, the burning of Athens, the battles of Marathon and Salamis and Plataea. These events were real and consequential. But they occupied a relatively small slice of Persian history and an even smaller slice of Persian geography. To understand the Achaemenid Empire only through its wars with Greece is like understanding the Roman Empire only through its conflicts with Carthage - illuminating in one direction, blind in almost every other.

There is also a tendency to read Persia as monolithic - a single imperial will expressed through a single royal voice. The reality was far more layered. The empire's genius lay precisely in its tolerance of difference. Conquered peoples were generally permitted to keep their languages, their religious practices, and their local customs, provided they paid their taxes and kept the peace. Cyrus famously allowed the Jewish exiles in Babylon to return to their homeland and rebuild their temple - an act recorded in the Hebrew Bible and confirmed by Persian sources. This was not sentimentality. It was policy. And it was a policy that worked.

What This Book Covers

This is a civilization-focused history, not a parade of kings. Rulers matter here - Cyrus, Darius, Xerxes, and the others who shaped the empire's trajectory - but they appear as products of a civilization, not as its sole content. The people who built the roads, administered the satrapies, traded across the empire's vast internal networks, practiced their faiths, and raised their families in the shadow of Persepolis: they are part of this story too.

The timeframe runs from the early Persians - the tribal and cultural foundations that preceded the empire - through the full arc of the Achaemenid dynasty, which endured from 550 BC until Alexander of Macedon extinguished it in 330 BC. Two centuries of continuous imperial history, punctuated by expansion, internal crisis, administrative innovation, and cultural achievement. More than enough to fill a book.

What this history does not attempt is exhaustiveness. The Achaemenid Empire was enormous, and a truly comprehensive account of every campaign, every satrap, every administrative reform would require multiple volumes and a tolerance for detail that most readers - reasonably - do not have. The goal here is understanding, not inventory. By the end of this book, you should have a clear sense of how the empire was built, how it functioned, why it lasted as long as it did, and what it left behind.

How to Use This Book

A few practical notes before we begin, because the ancient world comes with complications worth addressing directly.

On names: Persian history sits at the intersection of multiple naming traditions, and this creates genuine confusion. The same ruler might appear as Khshayarsha in Old Persian, Ahasuerus in Hebrew, and Xerxes in Greek. This book generally uses the Greek forms of names - Cyrus, Darius, Xerxes - because they are the most familiar to modern readers and appear most frequently in the sources most readers will encounter elsewhere. Where the Persian form is particularly illuminating or commonly used in scholarship, it will be introduced alongside the Greek version.

On maps: Several maps appear throughout the book to help orient you within the empire's geography. Ancient borders were not fixed lines on a page - they shifted with military campaigns, diplomatic arrangements, and the practical limits of administrative reach. Read the maps as approximations of political reality, not precise boundaries. Pay particular attention to the relationship between geography and governance: the empire's road systems, its river valleys, and its mountain ranges all shaped how power actually moved across this vast territory.

On what makes this different: Most popular histories of ancient Persia either retell the Greek wars or focus narrowly on royal biography. This book tries to hold a wider lens - to treat the Achaemenid Empire as a civilization worth understanding on its own terms, with its own internal logic, its own achievements, and its own contradictions. That means spending time on administration and culture alongside military campaigns. It means taking Persian sources seriously alongside Greek ones. And it means resisting the temptation to treat the empire's eventual fall as the point of the whole story.

Quick Summary

- The Achaemenid Empire, founded by Cyrus the Great in 550 BC, lasted until 330 BC - over two centuries of continuous imperial history.

- At its peak around 500 BC, the empire may have governed between 17 and 35 million people across three continents.

- Most popular accounts of ancient Persia are filtered through Greek sources, which emphasize conflict with Greece at the expense of the empire's broader civilization.

- Persian governance was notable for its tolerance of cultural, religious, and linguistic diversity - a deliberate policy, not an accident.

- Key rulers - Cyrus, Darius I, and Xerxes I - each shaped the empire in distinct ways, from its founding and expansion to its administrative consolidation and military reach.

- This book uses Greek name forms for familiarity, but engages with Persian and other ancient sources throughout.

- The goal is to understand Persia as a civilization, not simply as an antagonist in someone else's story.

Two and a half millennia have passed since Cyrus rode out of the Iranian plateau and began assembling the ancient world's largest empire. The civilization he founded shaped the cultures, governance structures, and religious landscapes of every major power that followed it - Greek, Roman, Islamic. Understanding Persia is not an exercise in antiquarianism. It is a way of understanding how the world we inherited was made. That story begins, as so many do, with a single remarkable man and the world he was determined to change.

PART 1
ROOTS OF A CIVILIZATION

Chapter 1
Before the Empire -
The World of Early Persia

Long before Cyrus the Great rode out of the highlands to reshape the ancient world, the Iranian plateau was already old. Civilizations had risen and fallen across its sun-baked plains and mountain passes for thousands of years, leaving behind pottery shards, administrative tablets, and the faint outlines of cities that once hummed with commerce and ambition. To understand the Persian Empire, you have to begin here - not with kings and conquests, but with the land itself, and with the peoples who learned, generation by generation, how to live on it.

This chapter reaches back before the Achaemenid dynasty, before the name "Persia" carried any imperial weight at all. It traces the migrations of the Indo-Iranian peoples who would eventually become the Persians and Medes, examines the formidable civilization of Elam that preceded and shaped them, and surveys the physical geography of the Iranian plateau - because in the ancient world, geography was destiny. The mountains, rivers, and deserts of Iran did not merely frame history; they determined it.

What emerges from this deep prehistory is not a simple story of one people replacing another. It is something more interesting: a layered world of migrations, cultural borrowings, trade networks, and competing powers, all of which deposited sediment - cultural, linguistic, political - that the later Persian Empire would draw upon when it finally arrived.

The Land That Shaped Everything

Stand on the Iranian plateau today and you immediately understand why it produced tough, adaptable peoples. The plateau sits at an average elevation of roughly 900 meters above sea level, ringed by mountain ranges that act as both barriers and gateways. To the north, the Alborz Mountains run along the Caspian coast; to the west, the Zagros range forms a dramatic spine of ridges and valleys that separates the plateau from Mesopotamia. To the south and east, the land drops toward the Persian Gulf and opens into the vast, punishing deserts of the interior - the Dasht-e Kavir and the Dasht-e Lut, two of the most inhospitable stretches of terrain on earth.

This geography created a world of contrasts. The Zagros foothills received enough rainfall to support agriculture and dense settlement. The plateau's interior was far less forgiving, demanding either nomadic adaptation or careful management of scarce water through underground irrigation channels known as *qanats*. The Persian Gulf coastline, meanwhile, offered access to maritime trade routes that connected the Iranian world to Mesopotamia, the Arabian Peninsula, and beyond.

Geography also meant that the Iranian plateau was never truly isolated. It sat at a crossroads. Peoples, goods, and ideas moved through it constantly - from Central Asia in the east, from Mesopotamia in the west, from the steppes of the north. Every civilization that took root here did so in conversation, and often in conflict, with neighbors near and far. That pattern of exchange and collision would define Iranian history for millennia.

The Indo-Iranian Migrations

Sometime in the second millennium BCE - historians and archaeologists continue to debate the precise timing - groups of semi-nomadic pastoralists began moving out of the Eurasian steppes and into the lands to the south and east. These were the Indo-Iranians, speakers of an early branch of the Indo-European language family, and their migrations would eventually carry their descendants across a vast arc of territory stretching from the Indian subcontinent to the edges of Mesopotamia.

The Iranian branch of this migration brought peoples who would eventually be known by names familiar from later history: the Medes, the Persians, the Parthians, the Bactrians. They were not a single unified group marching under one banner. They were a collection of related tribes, sharing broadly similar languages, religious practices, and ways of life, who filtered into the Iranian plateau over centuries rather than decades.

What they brought with them mattered enormously. Their language - Old Iranian, in its various dialects - would become the foundation of Persian, one of the great literary and administrative languages of the ancient world. Their religious traditions, centered on the worship of natural forces and a pantheon of gods, would eventually evolve into Zoroastrianism, the faith that would give the Persian Empire much of its moral and cosmological framework. And their social organization, built around tribal kinship and pastoral mobility, would shape the political structures of the kingdoms they eventually founded.

Their arrival did not happen in a vacuum. The Iranian plateau was already inhabited. And the civilization they encountered there - older, more urbanized, and more administratively sophisticated than anything the newcomers had yet produced - was Elam.

Elam: The Civilization That Came First

Elam is one of history's underappreciated giants. Centered on the lowland plains of what is now southwestern Iran - particularly the region around the city of Susa - Elamite civilization flourished for roughly two thousand years before the Persians emerged as a distinct political force. At its height, Elam was a major power in the ancient Near East, capable of challenging Mesopotamia's greatest kingdoms and projecting influence across a wide region.

Susa, Elam's most important city, sat at a natural meeting point between the Iranian highlands and the Mesopotamian lowlands. This location made it both strategically valuable and culturally permeable. Ideas, goods, and people flowed through Susa in both directions, and the city accumulated layers of cultural influence the way a river delta accumulates sediment - slowly, continuously, and in ways that are difficult to fully separate afterward.

Between Elam and Mesopotamia, the relationship was never simple. Sometimes it was commercial, sometimes diplomatic, sometimes violently competitive. Around 2200 BCE, the Akkadian king Sargon invaded Susa, an event that introduced a fresh wave of Mesopotamian cultural influence into Elamite society. Yet Elam was never simply absorbed. It retained its own language - unrelated to any known language family, a remarkable linguistic isolate - its own administrative traditions, and its own political identity. Elam borrowed from Mesopotamia selectively, on its own terms.

Life Inside Elamite Society

What was daily life like in Elam? Administrative documents recovered from Haft Tappeh, an important Elamite site, offer a rare and surprisingly detailed window into the society's inner workings. Among the most striking findings is evidence of women's active participation in the economy. Records from the second half of the second millennium BCE document women in roles that suggest meaningful socio-economic agency - not merely as dependents or household figures, but as participants in the administrative and economic life of their communities.

This kind of evidence matters because it complicates the picture of ancient Near Eastern societies as uniformly patriarchal and rigidly hierarchical. Elamite society had its own internal logic, its own ways of organizing labor and distributing resources, and those ways were not simply copies of Mesopotamian models.

Elam was also a society deeply embedded in regional trade networks. Archaeological surveys of Bushehr province along the Persian Gulf coast have revealed evidence of sustained exchange between the southern and northern Gulf during the Elamite period. Goods moved along these routes - raw materials, finished products, and almost certainly ideas and people as well. The Elamite world was connected to a wider commercial universe that stretched across the Gulf and into the broader ancient Near East.

The Medes: First Among the Iranian Peoples

As the Indo-Iranian migrations settled into the plateau and the newcomers began to establish more permanent communities, distinct political identities started to crystallize. Among the most significant of these early Iranian peoples were the Medes, who established themselves in the northwestern part of the plateau, in the region around the city of Ecbatana - modern Hamadan.

The Medes represent the first Iranian people to organize themselves into a recognizable kingdom capable of projecting significant military and political power. Their rise was partly a response to external pressure: the Assyrian Empire, based in northern Mesopotamia, was aggressively expanding during the early first millennium BCE, and the peoples of the Zagros region faced repeated Assyrian campaigns. The Medes coalesced, at least in part, as a defensive and then offensive response to that pressure.

By the late seventh century BCE, the Median kingdom had become powerful enough to play a decisive role in the destruction of the Assyrian Empire itself - a seismic event in ancient Near Eastern history that cleared the way for new powers to emerge. Among those emerging powers were the Persians, a related Iranian people settled further to the south and east, in the region known as Persis - the heartland of what would become the Persian Empire.

The Neo-Elamite Period and the Transition

Between roughly 1000 and 525 BCE, Elam entered what historians call the Neo-Elamite period - a phase marked by continued political activity, cultural production, and interaction with the increasingly powerful Iranian peoples moving through and settling the plateau. This was not a period of simple Elamite decline. Neo-Elamite rulers remained significant players in regional politics, sometimes allying with Mesopotamian powers, sometimes opposing them, and always negotiating their position in a rapidly changing world.

The Elamite legacy did not disappear when the Achaemenid Persians rose to dominance after 525 BCE. Susa became one of the great royal capitals of the Persian Empire. Elamite administrative traditions influenced Persian bureaucratic practice. The cultural and institutional inheritance of Elam flowed directly into the civilization that would eventually produce Cyrus, Darius, and Xerxes.

Here lies one of the most important and often overlooked points about the Persian Empire: it did not emerge from nowhere. It was built on foundations that had been laid over centuries - by Elamite administrators, by Indo-Iranian migrants, by Median warriors, and by the countless unnamed people who traded goods along the Persian Gulf, farmed the Zagros foothills, and passed their languages and beliefs to their children.

Key Figures and Moments

Sargon of Akkad stands as one of the earliest named figures to leave a direct mark on the Iranian world. His invasion of Susa around 2200 BCE was not merely a military event - it was a cultural collision that accelerated the exchange of ideas between Mesopotamia and Elam, shaping the development of both civilizations for centuries to come.

The Elamite administrators of Haft Tappeh, though unnamed in the surviving record, left behind documents that illuminate the texture of a sophisticated society - one in which women held recognized economic roles and the machinery of governance extended into the details of daily life.

The Median kings, whose names appear in later sources, represent the first chapter of Iranian political history in the recognizable sense - rulers commanding armies, negotiating with empires, and building the institutional frameworks that the Persians would later inherit and transform.

What the Archaeology Tells Us

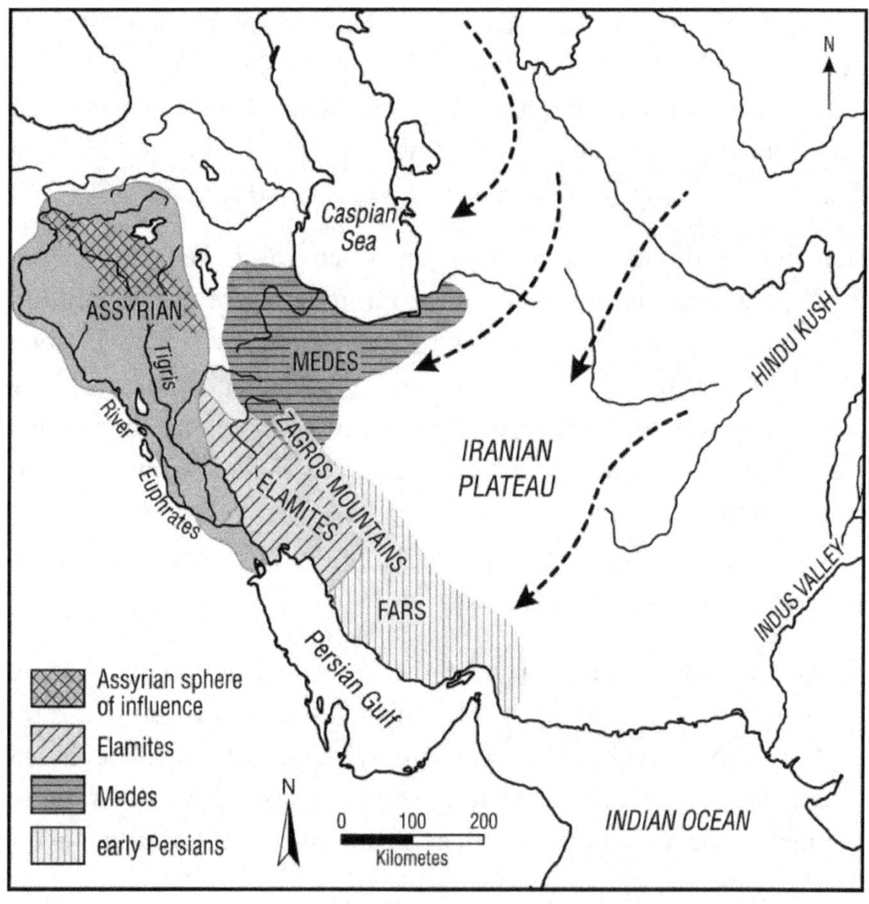

Peoples of the Iranian Plateau, c. 1000–700 BCE

The material record of pre-Achaemenid Iran is uneven but genuinely revealing. Archaeological surveys of Bushehr province have documented human activity across multiple periods - from the Chalcolithic era through the Elamite kingdom and into the Achaemenid age - confirming that the Persian Gulf coast was not a peripheral backwater but an active zone of regional exchange. Pottery, trade goods, and settlement patterns all point to a world in motion, connected across considerable distances by commerce and cultural contact.

Haft Tappeh's administrative tablets remind us that literacy and bureaucratic organization were not Achaemenid inventions. They were inherited tools, refined over centuries by Elamite scribes working in a tradition that stretched back to the earliest urban civilizations of the ancient Near East.

The archaeological picture is incomplete - much of the Iranian plateau remains underexplored, and political circumstances have limited fieldwork in recent decades. But what exists is enough to sketch the outlines of a rich, complex world that preceded the empire.

Quick Summary

- The Iranian plateau's geography - mountain ranges, arid interior, and Gulf coastline - shaped the development of all the civilizations that arose there, creating a world defined by both isolation and connectivity.

- Indo-Iranian peoples migrated onto the plateau during the second millennium BCE, bringing with them the linguistic and religious traditions that would eventually become distinctly Persian.

- Elam dominated the region for roughly two thousand years, centered on Susa and maintaining complex relationships - commercial, diplomatic, and military - with Mesopotamia.

- Sargon of Akkad's invasion of Susa around 2200 BCE introduced Mesopotamian cultural influences into Elamite society, illustrating the deep interconnection between these two worlds.

- Administrative documents from Haft Tappeh reveal that Elamite society was sophisticated and internally complex, with women playing documented socio-economic roles.

- Archaeological evidence from Bushehr province confirms the Persian Gulf coast's importance as a zone of regional trade and exchange across multiple historical periods.

- The Medes were the first Iranian people to organize a significant kingdom, and their political and military legacy directly shaped the conditions from which the Persian Empire would emerge.

- Elamite administrative traditions, urban infrastructure, and cultural practices did not vanish with the rise of the Achaemenids - they were absorbed and transformed, becoming part of the empire's foundation.

Great empires are never truly created from scratch. They are assembled - from inherited institutions, borrowed ideas, absorbed peoples, and accumulated experience. When Cyrus the Great began his conquests in the sixth century BCE, he was not building on empty ground. He was standing on the shoulders of Elamite scribes, Median warriors, and Indo-Iranian migrants who had spent a thousand years turning a difficult, beautiful plateau into something that could, at last, sustain an empire. How that empire actually came together is where the story turns next.

Chapter 2
The Rise of the Persians

Before there was an empire, there was a plateau.

Stretching across what is now modern Iran, the Iranian Plateau sits at the crossroads of ancient worlds - a vast, windswept expanse of mountains, salt deserts, and fertile river valleys where nomadic peoples had wandered, settled, and competed for centuries. Out of this rugged terrain, two related peoples emerged who would, together, reshape the ancient world: the Medes and the Persians. Their story is not simply one of conquest and domination. It is a story of how scattered tribes coalesced into something larger, how cultures blended and borrowed until the line between conqueror and conquered blurred, and how a people could rise from the margins of history to stand at its very center.

That transformation begins with the early identity of the Persian people - who they were, where they came from, and how they organized themselves before the age of empire. It then turns to the relationship between the Persians and their more powerful neighbors, the Medes, whose shadow loomed large over Persian development. And it follows the arc of that relationship to its dramatic turning point: the moment in 550 BC when a Persian chief named Cyrus II rode out of the south and changed everything.

A People Taking Shape: Early Persian Identity

Pinning down the origins of the ancient Persians is a task that humbles even the most careful historian. They did not arrive fully formed on the stage of history. Like most of the great civilizations of the ancient world, they emerged gradually - through migration, adaptation, and the slow accumulation of cultural identity across generations.

The Persians were an Indo-European people, part of the broader wave of migrations that swept across Eurasia in the second millennium BC. They spoke an early form of what would become Old Persian, a language belonging to the Iranian branch of the Indo-European family - a linguistic cousin to Sanskrit in the east and the ancestral tongues of Greece and Rome in the west. Language was more than communication; it was identity. The shared tongue connected Persian-speaking communities across vast distances, binding them to a common heritage even when political unity remained elusive.

Their early social structure was tribal. Leadership was personal and earned - chiefs commanded loyalty through demonstrated strength, wisdom, and the ability to protect and provide for their people. Kinship networks formed the backbone of political life, with extended family clans operating as the fundamental unit of society. Loyalty ran along bloodlines before it ran toward any abstract notion of statehood.

Settled primarily in the region known as Persis - roughly corresponding to the modern Iranian province of Fars - the early Persians were neither the most powerful nor the most prominent people on the plateau. That distinction, for much of the early first millennium BC, belonged to their northern neighbors.

In the Shadow of the Medes

To understand the rise of the Persians, you first have to understand the Medes - because for a long time, the Persians lived in their shadow.

The Medes occupied the northwestern reaches of the Iranian Plateau, centered around the region of Media, which lay to the north and west of Persis. By the seventh century BC, they were a formidable power. Where the Persians were still organized around tribal structures, the Medes had developed a more consolidated political order - one capable of projecting military force across considerable distances and of challenging the great empires of Mesopotamia.

The relationship between the Medes and the Persians was not simply one of domination and submission, though there were certainly elements of both. The two peoples shared deep cultural and linguistic roots. They spoke related Iranian languages, worshipped similar deities, and organized their societies along broadly comparable lines. In many respects, the Medes and the Persians were kin - different branches of the same ancient family tree, separated by geography and circumstance more than by fundamental culture.

That kinship made the political relationship between them all the more complex. Persian chiefs operated within a world where Median power was the dominant regional force. Persian leaders managed this reality carefully, sometimes submitting to Median authority, sometimes maneuvering for greater autonomy, always aware that the balance of power on the plateau was not fixed.

What the Persians absorbed from this proximity was as important as what they resisted. Median administrative practices, military organization, and courtly culture all left their mark on Persian development. The Persians were not passive recipients - they adapted, refined, and eventually surpassed what they had inherited. But the inheritance itself was real and significant. The Achaemenid Empire that would later astonish the ancient world did not spring from nothing. It grew, in part, from seeds planted during the long years of Persian-Median interaction.

Language, Culture, and the Architecture of Leadership

What distinguished the early Persians as a people was not military power - they did not yet have that in abundance - but a set of cultural and organizational characteristics that would prove remarkably durable.

Old Persian, the language of the early Persian elite, was more than a means of communication. It carried within it a worldview - a set of values, relationships, and assumptions about authority and order.

Persian inscriptions from the Achaemenid period later reveal a culture deeply concerned with truth, justice, and the proper ordering of the world. The concept of *arta* - a term roughly translatable as "truth" or "cosmic order" - appears repeatedly in Persian religious and royal contexts. This was not mere rhetoric. It reflected a genuine cultural preoccupation with the idea that good rulership meant maintaining order against chaos, justice against falsehood.

Leadership among the early Persians was structured around this idea. A chief was not simply a warlord. He was expected to embody qualities of wisdom and fairness alongside martial prowess. The tribal structures that organized Persian society placed real demands on leaders - loyalty was given, not assumed, and it could be withdrawn. A chief who failed his people, who proved unjust or incompetent, risked losing the very networks of kinship and obligation that sustained his authority.

This created a particular kind of political culture - one that valued personal charisma and demonstrated virtue in leadership, not merely inherited rank. It was a culture that would, in the right hands, prove extraordinarily generative. When Cyrus II emerged from Persis in the sixth century BC, he did not simply conquer. He persuaded. He incorporated. He ruled in a manner that drew on deep Persian traditions of what legitimate leadership looked like - and that capacity would define the empire he built.

The Turning Point: Cyrus and the Fall of Astyages

By the mid-sixth century BC, the political map of the ancient Near East was dominated by a handful of great powers: Babylon in Mesopotamia, Lydia in western Anatolia, Egypt along the Nile, and Media on the Iranian Plateau. Persia was not among them. Then, in 550 BC, everything changed.

Cyrus II - later called "the Great," a title he would earn many times over - was the chief of the Persian Achaemenid clan. He ruled Persis as a vassal under Median authority, nominally subject to the Median king Astyages. What drove him to rebellion against his overlord is not entirely clear from the surviving sources, but the outcome is beyond dispute. Cyrus rose against Astyages, and Astyages fell.

The defeat of the Median king was not simply a military victory. Ancient accounts suggest that Astyages faced significant internal opposition - that Median nobles and even elements of his own army turned against him, a sign that his rule had generated resentment and discontent. Cyrus moved into this fracture with devastating effect. Astyages was captured. Media was subjugated. And the man who had been a vassal chief on the margins of great-power politics suddenly stood at the center of the ancient world.

What Cyrus did next revealed the character of the empire he intended to build. Rather than treating the Medes as a conquered people to be humiliated and exploited, he integrated them. Median nobles retained positions of influence. Median administrative practices were preserved and incorporated. The Persian court absorbed Median courtly traditions - dress, ceremony, protocol - to such a degree that later Greek observers sometimes struggled to distinguish between the two peoples, referring to both simply as "Medes."

This was not weakness. It was policy - and it was brilliant. By treating the Medes as partners rather than subjects, Cyrus transformed a military conquest into a political foundation. The Achaemenid Empire that emerged from 550 BC was, from its very beginning, a composite creation: Persian in its ruling dynasty and core identity, but Median in much of its administrative structure and cultural texture.

What the Merger Made

The integration of the Medes and the Persians was one of the formative events in the history of the ancient world, though it rarely receives the attention it deserves.

From the Persian side, the absorption of Media brought administrative sophistication, established networks of governance across the plateau, and the prestige of a people who had, within living memory, been a great power in their own right. From the Median side, incorporation into the Achaemenid project offered continuity, survival, and - for those who chose to embrace it - participation in something growing rapidly into a force far larger than either people had been alone.

The cultural synthesis that resulted was neither purely Persian nor purely Median. It was something new - a hybrid political culture capable of governing vast territories and diverse populations. This capacity for synthesis, for incorporating rather than simply dominating, would become the defining characteristic of Achaemenid rule. Cyrus applied it to the Medes in 550 BC, and his successors would apply it, with varying degrees of success, to Babylonians, Lydians, Egyptians, and dozens of other peoples across the empire's expanding reach.

Media itself remained significant long after the conquest. The region's wealth, its strategic position, and its population of experienced administrators and soldiers made it a cornerstone of the Achaemenid imperial system. When Alexander the Great swept through the region in 330 BC, occupying Media as part of his extraordinary campaign against the Persian Empire, he was claiming one of the most valuable prizes in the ancient world. After his death, the territory was divided among his successors - southern Media passing to the Macedonian commander Peithon, while northern Media became the semi-independent kingdom of Atropatene, established by Atropates, a former general of the last Achaemenid king, Darius III. The name Atropatene survives, transformed, in the modern name Azerbaijan - a small linguistic echo of a world that has otherwise largely vanished.

From Tribes to Power: The Larger Pattern

The story of early Persian identity and the Persian-Median relationship reveals a pattern that recurs across the ancient world: the transition from tribal organization to imperial power is rarely a simple matter of one strong people overwhelming weaker ones. It is almost always more complicated - more dependent on cultural absorption, political flexibility, and the capacity to make allies out of former rivals.

The Persians did not rise because they were simply more powerful than the Medes. In raw military terms, the Medes had been the dominant force for generations. The Persians rose because, at a critical moment, they produced a leader in Cyrus II who understood that conquest alone does not build an empire. What builds an empire is the ability to make the conquered feel that their participation in the new order is worthwhile - that their traditions will be respected, their elites accommodated, their identities preserved within a larger whole.

That insight, rooted in Persian cultural traditions of just and legitimate leadership, was the true foundation of Achaemenid power. The military victories came first, but the empire was built on what followed them.

Quick Summary

- The early Persians were an Indo-European people settled in the region of Persis on the Iranian Plateau, organized around tribal structures with leadership based on personal merit and kinship loyalty.

- Old Persian language and the cultural concept of *arta* (truth/cosmic order) shaped Persian values around just and legitimate rulership from an early period.

- The Medes were the dominant power on the Iranian Plateau before the Persians, and the two peoples shared deep cultural and linguistic roots that made their later integration more natural.

- In 550 BC, Cyrus II defeated the Median king Astyages, ending Median dominance and establishing Persian supremacy - a turning point that launched the Achaemenid Empire.

- Rather than suppressing the Medes, Cyrus integrated them into his new imperial structure, preserving Median administrative practices and incorporating Median elites - a policy of inclusion that became the hallmark of Achaemenid rule.

- The merger of Persian and Median cultures produced a hybrid political civilization capable of governing vast and diverse territories.

- Media remained strategically vital for centuries, eventually falling to Alexander the Great in 330 BC and later fragmenting into successor territories, including the kingdom of Atropatene - whose name survives in modern Azerbaijan.

The rise of the Persians from plateau tribes to imperial masters was not an accident of geography or a simple product of military force. It was the result of cultural depth, political intelligence, and a particular understanding of what power requires to endure. Cyrus II did not just defeat his enemies - he reimagined what it meant to rule them. That reimagining would echo forward through centuries of Persian history, shaping an empire that, at its height, would govern more of the known world than any state before it. Whether the generations that followed could sustain what he had begun is another question entirely.

PART 2
THE MAKING OF AN EMPIRE

Chapter 3
Cyrus the Great - Founder of a New Order

When Cyrus of Persia rode into Babylon in 539 BCE, he did something no conqueror of that city had ever quite managed: he was welcomed.

That single fact tells you almost everything you need to know about what made Cyrus the Great different. In an age when empire-building meant burning cities, enslaving populations, and erasing the names of defeated kings, Cyrus built something new - not just a larger empire, but a different kind of empire entirely. He conquered more territory than almost anyone before him, yet his most enduring weapon was not the sword. It was the idea that a ruler could win loyalty by granting dignity rather than demanding submission.

What follows traces the arc of that achievement: from Cyrus's unlikely rise in the highlands of Persia, through his stunning campaigns against Media, Lydia, and Babylon, to the governing philosophy that held it all together. At the center of that philosophy sits one of the ancient world's most remarkable objects - a small clay cylinder, barely the size of a human forearm, inscribed with words that still resonate more than two and a half millennia later.

A King from the Margins

Persia, in the early sixth century BCE, was not the center of anything. It was a tributary kingdom on the edges of the Median Empire, a highland territory whose rulers paid homage to the Medes and whose ambitions were, by necessity, kept quiet. Cyrus came to the Persian throne around 559 BCE, inheriting a kingdom that was, by the standards of the ancient Near East, a minor player.

What happened next unfolded with a speed that still surprises historians.

Within a generation, Cyrus had dismantled the Median Empire, absorbed the fabulously wealthy kingdom of Lydia, and brought the ancient city of Babylon - the greatest metropolis of the ancient world - under Persian control. He did all of this between roughly 559 and 539 BCE, a span of just two decades. By the time of his death in 530 BCE, he ruled over a domain stretching from the Aegean coast in the west to the edges of Central Asia in the east. It was, at that point, the largest empire the world had ever seen.

But the scale of the conquest is almost less interesting than the method.

Defeating the Medes: The First Move

Cyrus's first major campaign targeted the Median Empire - the very power that had dominated Persia for generations. The Medes, under their king Astyages, controlled a vast territory across what is now northwestern Iran and eastern Anatolia. They were formidable. They were also, as it turned out, deeply unpopular with their own commanders.

When Cyrus moved against Astyages, the Median army reportedly turned on their own king. Ancient sources, including the Greek historian Herodotus, describe Median generals defecting to Cyrus rather than fighting him - a pattern that would repeat itself across his campaigns. Whether through military pressure, political maneuvering, or genuine popular appeal, Cyrus had a gift for making his enemies' alliances collapse from within.

By defeating Media, Cyrus did not simply win a war. He inherited an empire. He absorbed Median territory, Median administrative structures, and - crucially - Median prestige. Rather than humiliating the defeated Medes, he incorporated them into his new order. This was not mercy for its own sake. It was strategy. A conquered people who feel respected are far cheaper to govern than a conquered people waiting for the chance to revolt.

Lydia and the Wealth of Croesus

If the defeat of Media announced Cyrus as a serious power, his conquest of Lydia announced him to the wider world.

Lydia, in western Anatolia, was ruled by Croesus - a king so legendarily wealthy that his name became a byword for riches lasting to this day. Lydia had grown rich partly through trade and partly through an innovation that would reshape the ancient economy: the minting of standardized coinage. Croesus's gold and silver coins circulated across the Mediterranean world, and his treasury was the envy of every king from Greece to Mesopotamia.

Croesus, alarmed by Cyrus's rapid expansion, sought allies and consulted oracles. Herodotus records that the Oracle at Delphi told him that if he crossed the Halys River to attack Cyrus, he would destroy a great empire. Croesus took this as encouragement. He crossed the river. The empire he destroyed was his own.

The campaign unfolded around 546 BCE. After an inconclusive initial battle, Croesus retreated to his capital at Sardis, expecting to regroup over the winter. Cyrus did not give him the winter. He pursued immediately, besieged Sardis, and captured the city. Croesus was taken prisoner. Lydia fell.

What Cyrus gained was not just territory. He gained access to the Greek cities along the Aegean coast, to the trade networks of the Mediterranean, and to the administrative sophistication of a kingdom that had been managing complex commercial relationships for generations. Once again, he absorbed rather than destroyed.

The Fall of Babylon

Nothing in Cyrus's career, however, matched the symbolic and strategic weight of Babylon.

By 539 BCE, Babylon was ancient even by ancient standards. It had been a center of civilization for more than a thousand years. Its walls were legendary - described by Herodotus as among the greatest structures in the known world. Its temples, particularly the great ziggurat known as Etemenanki, were monuments to a religious tradition stretching back to the earliest days of Mesopotamian civilization. To hold Babylon was to hold the symbolic heart of the Near East.

The city was ruled at this time by Nabonidus, a king who had managed to alienate large portions of his own population. He had neglected the cult of Marduk, Babylon's chief deity, in favor of the moon god Sin - a theological shift that infuriated the powerful priestly class. He had also spent years away from the city, leaving governance in the hands of his son Belshazzar. By the time Cyrus arrived, Babylon was a city whose king had lost the confidence of its most powerful institutions.

Cyrus moved against Babylon with military force, but the city's fall owed as much to internal fracture as to Persian arms. Persian forces defeated the Babylonian army at the Battle of Opis, and shortly afterward, Babylon itself was taken - reportedly with minimal resistance. Ancient accounts, including the Cyrus Cylinder, present the conquest as something close to a liberation. Marduk, the great god of Babylon, had chosen Cyrus as his instrument, the cylinder declares. The priests who had chafed under Nabonidus found in this framing a theology that suited them perfectly.

Whether the welcome was as universal as Persian sources suggest is a question historians continue to debate. But the political reality was clear: Cyrus entered Babylon not as a destroyer but as a restorer, and he was shrewd enough to present himself in exactly those terms.

The Cyrus Cylinder: A Ruler's Manifesto in Clay

Buried in the foundations of the Esagila Temple in Babylon, the Cyrus Cylinder is one of the most extraordinary objects to survive from the ancient world. Inscribed in cuneiform - the wedge-shaped script of Mesopotamian civilization - it is a small barrel-shaped clay cylinder, modest in size and staggering in significance.

The cylinder was discovered in the nineteenth century and now resides in the British Museum, though its contents have generated debate and admiration far beyond the walls of any single institution.

What does it say? The text presents Cyrus's conquest of Babylon as an act of divine will and humanitarian restoration. It describes Nabonidus as a ruler who had failed his people and offended the gods. It presents Cyrus as the chosen king of Marduk, welcomed by the population of Babylon with joy. And then it goes further.

The cylinder records that Cyrus allowed displaced peoples to return to their homelands and restored temples and religious practices that previous rulers had suppressed. It speaks of releasing people from burdens and hardships. These were not empty words - they corresponded to documented actions, including the famous decree that allowed the Jewish exiles in Babylon to return to Judea and rebuild their temple in Jerusalem. That decree is referenced in the Hebrew Bible, in the books of Ezra and Isaiah, where Cyrus is described in terms of extraordinary reverence - the only non-Jewish figure in the Hebrew scriptures to be called a messiah, an anointed one.

Some modern scholars have cautioned against reading the cylinder as a straightforward human rights document in the contemporary sense. It follows established Mesopotamian traditions of royal proclamation, and its language of liberation served clear political purposes - legitimizing Persian rule by casting it as divine favor rather than military conquest. But even accounting for the propagandistic dimension, the policies it describes were real, and their effects were felt by real people across the ancient Near East.

The cylinder is not a constitution. But it is evidence of a governing philosophy - one that recognized the practical wisdom of tolerance.

Governing an Empire of Many Peoples

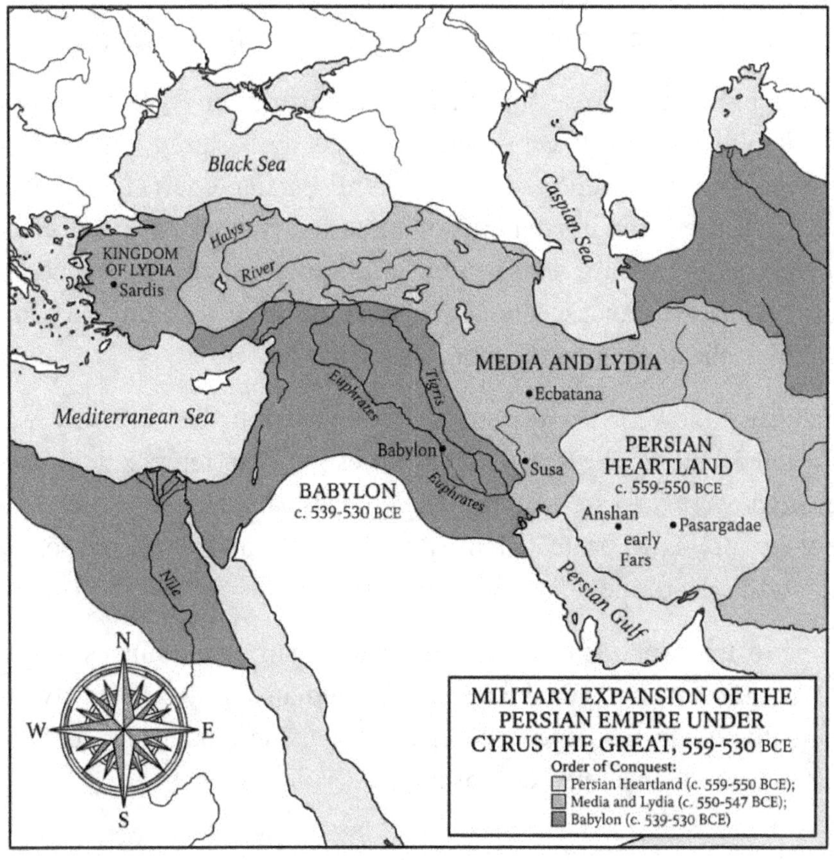

The expansion of Persia under Cyrus, 559–530 BCE

What Cyrus built was not simply a larger version of the empires that came before it. It was something structurally different.

Previous Near Eastern empires - Assyrian, Babylonian, Egyptian - had generally imposed their own culture, language, and religion on conquered peoples. The Assyrians in particular were notorious for mass deportations and the deliberate erasure of local identity. Cyrus moved in the opposite direction. He allowed conquered peoples to maintain their languages, their religions, and their local customs. He presented himself not as a foreign conqueror but as the legitimate successor to local traditions - as the chosen of Marduk in Babylon, as the heir to the Median kings, as a restorer rather than a destroyer.

This approach required sophisticated administration. Cyrus organized his empire into provinces, each governed by a satrap - a regional administrator who reported to the central Persian court. Local elites were often retained in positions of authority, provided they accepted Persian overlordship. This system allowed the empire to function across vast distances and enormous cultural diversity without requiring the constant application of military force.

Stability followed. Conquered peoples who felt their identity was respected had less reason to rebel. Priests whose temples had been restored were invested in the new order. Merchants whose trade routes were now protected by Persian arms had every reason to support Persian rule.

None of this was idealism. It was pragmatism of the highest order. But pragmatism and genuine respect for human dignity are not always mutually exclusive, and the legacy Cyrus left suggests that his approach contained elements of both.

Legacy: The Shape of What Came After

Cyrus died in 530 BCE, reportedly during a military campaign in the east. He left behind an empire that his successors - Cambyses, Darius, Xerxes - would expand still further, eventually stretching from Egypt to the borders of India. The administrative and philosophical framework he established shaped the Achaemenid Empire for two centuries.

His influence reached beyond Persia. Alexander the Great, who conquered the Achaemenid Empire in the 330s BCE, reportedly admired Cyrus deeply and visited his tomb at Pasargadae. The model of a ruler who governs through respect rather than terror was one that later conquerors and statesmen returned to again and again, whether or not they always managed to live up to it.

The Cyrus Cylinder itself has had a remarkable afterlife. In the twentieth century, it was adopted as a symbol by the last Shah of Iran, who used it to connect his regime to ancient Persian glory. More broadly, it has been cited in discussions of religious freedom, minority rights, and the ethics of governance - a two-and-a-half-thousand-year-old piece of clay that keeps finding new relevance.

Whether Cyrus deserves every element of the reputation that has accumulated around him is a fair question. Ancient sources - including the cylinder itself - were written to serve Persian interests, and the picture they paint is inevitably flattering. But the broad outlines of his approach are corroborated by multiple independent sources, including the Hebrew Bible, Greek historians, and the archaeological record. Something genuinely different was happening under his rule.

Quick Summary

- Cyrus the Great reigned from approximately 559 to 530 BCE and founded the Achaemenid Persian Empire.

- His rise began with the defeat of the Median Empire, whose own commanders reportedly defected rather than fight him.

- Around 546 BCE, he conquered Lydia, capturing the wealthy King Croesus and gaining access to the Aegean coast and Mediterranean trade networks.

- In 539 BCE, he took Babylon - the greatest city of the ancient world - with minimal resistance, aided by the unpopularity of the Babylonian king Nabonidus.

- The Cyrus Cylinder, inscribed in cuneiform and buried in the foundations of Babylon's Esagila Temple, records his policies of religious tolerance and the restoration of displaced peoples to their homelands.

- His decree allowing Jewish exiles to return to Judea is referenced in the Hebrew Bible, where he is described with extraordinary reverence.

- His governing philosophy - allowing conquered peoples to maintain their languages, religions, and customs - was both pragmatically effective and historically distinctive.

- His legacy shaped the Achaemenid Empire for two centuries and influenced later rulers, including Alexander the Great.

Cyrus the Great did not invent empire. But he reimagined what empire could mean - and in doing so, he set a standard that most of his successors, ancient and modern alike, have struggled to meet. The clay cylinder buried beneath a Babylonian temple was not just a record of conquest. It was a statement about power: that the most durable kind is the kind that people choose not to resist. That idea outlasted his empire by millennia. It may outlast all of us.

Chapter 4
Cambyses and the Expansion into Egypt

The Son Who Had to Prove Himself

When Cyrus the Great died in 530 BCE, he left behind the largest empire the world had ever seen - and a son who would spend his entire reign trying to prove he deserved it.

Cambyses II is one of history's most misunderstood rulers. Sandwiched between the towering legacy of his father and the administrative genius of Darius I, who came after him, Cambyses tends to appear in popular histories as little more than a cautionary tale - a brilliant conqueror undone by cruelty and madness. That portrait, drawn largely by the Greek historian Herodotus, has proven remarkably durable. It has also proven remarkably incomplete.

What actually happened during Cambyses' reign from 529 to 522 BCE is a story of strategic ambition, military innovation, and the brutal difficulty of holding together an empire that stretched from the Aegean coast to the edges of Central Asia. His conquest of Egypt in 525 BCE was not a reckless adventure. It was the culmination of a plan his father had begun and that Cambyses executed with considerable skill. Understanding his reign means setting aside the caricature and looking at what the evidence - including Egyptian sources that Herodotus never consulted - actually shows.

What follows traces Cambyses from his inheritance of the Persian throne to the banks of the Nile and beyond, through both his achievements and the limits that geography, logistics, and politics placed on even the most powerful ruler of the ancient world.

Inheriting the Impossible

Cyrus the Great had built something unprecedented. By the time of his death, the Achaemenid Persian Empire encompassed Persia, Media, Lydia, Babylon, and vast stretches of Central Asia. It was an empire of staggering diversity - dozens of languages, hundreds of local customs, and countless local power structures that Cyrus had learned to manage through a combination of military force and deliberate tolerance.

Cambyses inherited all of it. He also inherited the expectations that came with it.

No record suggests Cambyses was unprepared for power. He had served as a kind of regent in Babylon during his father's later campaigns, gaining administrative experience in one of the empire's most complex and culturally significant cities. When Cyrus died on campaign in the east, Cambyses assumed control without apparent crisis - a transition that, in the ancient world, was far from guaranteed.

One shadow fell over the succession almost immediately. Cambyses' younger brother, Bardiya - known to Greek sources as Smerdis - disappears from the historical record shortly after Cambyses took the throne. Later Persian accounts, including the famous Behistun Inscription commissioned by Darius I, claim that Cambyses had Bardiya killed secretly, fearing a rival claim to power. Whether this is true, or whether it was a convenient story told by the man who eventually seized the throne himself, remains genuinely contested. What is clear is that Bardiya's fate - real or fabricated - would haunt the final months of Cambyses' reign.

For now, though, Cambyses had a more immediate ambition. He turned his gaze west, toward the Nile.

The Plan His Father Left Behind

Egypt was the great prize of the ancient Near East. Wealthy, ancient, and militarily formidable, it sat at the crossroads of Africa and the Mediterranean world, controlling trade routes that fed empires. Cyrus had apparently recognized this. Evidence suggests he had already begun laying the groundwork for an Egyptian campaign before his death - gathering intelligence, cultivating contacts, and securing the naval resources that any serious invasion would require.

Cambyses picked up where his father left off, and he did so with methodical care.

One of his most important strategic moves was securing control of Phoenicia. The Phoenician city-states - Tyre, Sidon, and others along the Levantine coast - were the premier naval powers of the eastern Mediterranean. Their fleets were the finest available. By bringing Phoenicia firmly under Persian authority, Cambyses effectively neutralized Egypt's ability to contest the sea lanes and denied the Egyptians the naval support they might otherwise have called upon. Before a single Persian soldier crossed into Egyptian territory, Cambyses had already reshaped the strategic balance.

He also benefited from defections. Greek mercenaries who had served the Egyptian pharaoh Amasis reportedly provided intelligence about Egyptian defenses. A former Egyptian naval commander named Polycrates - the sources here are somewhat tangled - may have offered assistance as well. Cambyses was building a coalition, not simply marching an army.

By 525 BCE, the preparations were complete. The Persian army moved toward Egypt's northeastern frontier, and the two empires met at a place called Pelusium.

The Battle of Pelusium

Pelusium sat at the eastern edge of the Nile Delta, guarding the most direct land route into Egypt. It was the obvious place for a decisive confrontation, and both sides knew it.

What happened there has become one of antiquity's more striking military anecdotes. According to later accounts, Cambyses deployed an unusual psychological weapon against the Egyptian defenders: cats. The Egyptians held cats as sacred animals, associated with the goddess Bastet, and were deeply reluctant to harm them. Persian soldiers allegedly carried cats - or images of cats - into battle, knowing the Egyptians would hesitate to strike for fear of committing sacrilege.

Whether this account is literally true or embellished in the retelling, the underlying point is significant. Cambyses and his commanders understood Egyptian culture well enough to exploit it. This was not a blunt invasion. It was a campaign informed by intelligence, cultural awareness, and psychological calculation.

The battle itself was a decisive Persian victory. Egyptian forces broke, and the road to Memphis - Egypt's ancient capital - lay open. The new pharaoh, Psamtik III, who had only recently succeeded his father Amasis, attempted to rally resistance, but the momentum had shifted irreversibly. Memphis fell. Psamtik III was captured. Egypt, one of the oldest civilizations on earth, passed under Persian rule.

Ruling the Gift of the Nile

Conquest and governance are different arts, and Cambyses understood the distinction. His initial approach to ruling Egypt was notably conciliatory - a strategy that echoed his father's famous tolerance in Babylon and elsewhere.

Cambyses adopted Egyptian royal titles and presented himself as a legitimate pharaoh rather than a foreign conqueror. He participated in

Egyptian religious ceremonies and made offerings at Egyptian temples. Contemporary Egyptian inscriptions from this period do not describe him as a tyrant or a destroyer. Some Egyptian priests and officials appear to have cooperated with the new administration without obvious coercion.

This matters because it directly contradicts the portrait that Herodotus painted roughly a century later. In Herodotus' account, Cambyses was a man of violent instability - he allegedly stabbed the sacred Apis bull in a fit of impiety, mocked Egyptian religious customs, and behaved with erratic cruelty throughout his time in Egypt. Herodotus presents these acts as evidence of madness, even suggesting that Cambyses was literally insane.

Egyptian sources tell a different story. Archaeological evidence indicates that the Apis bull Herodotus claimed Cambyses killed actually died of natural causes during this period, with proper burial rites observed. Inscriptions show Cambyses making the expected ritual offerings. The picture that emerges from the ground is of a ruler who, at least initially, worked within Egyptian religious and political frameworks rather than against them.

Why the discrepancy? Herodotus was writing from Greek sources, many of them hostile to Persia, and his Egyptian informants may have had their own reasons for emphasizing Persian impiety. The image of Cambyses as a mad, sacrilegious tyrant served particular narrative purposes - for Greeks wary of Persian power, for Egyptians who resented foreign rule, and perhaps most of all for Darius I, who needed to justify his own seizure of the throne by casting his predecessor as unfit to rule.

History, as always, was written by those who survived.

Ambitions Beyond Egypt

Egypt was not enough. Having secured the Nile Delta and established Persian authority over one of the ancient world's most storied civilizations, Cambyses began planning further campaigns to extend Persian reach deeper into Africa and the western Mediterranean.

Three expeditions were contemplated or initiated. The first targeted the kingdom of Kush, in what is now Sudan - referred to in ancient sources as Ethiopia. The second aimed at the Oasis of Amon, deep in the Libyan desert, home to a famous oracle. The third, most ambitious of all, was directed against Carthage, the powerful Phoenician colony on the North African coast that had grown into a commercial empire of its own.

None of these campaigns succeeded as planned.

The Kushite expedition ran into the oldest enemy of armies: logistics. Persian supply lines stretched to their breaking point across the harsh terrain south of Egypt. According to Herodotus, soldiers were reduced to eating pack animals and then, in desperation, each other - though such accounts from ancient sources should be treated with appropriate skepticism. What is clear is that the campaign did not achieve its objectives and turned back before reaching its target.

The expedition toward the Oasis of Amon met an even more dramatic fate. A Persian force reportedly disappeared in the desert, swallowed by a sandstorm. Whether this account is literally accurate or represents a later mythologization of a military failure, the campaign produced no tangible results.

Carthage never materialized as a target at all. Cambyses' Phoenician fleet, the backbone of any western Mediterranean campaign, refused to attack a city that Phoenicians themselves regarded as a colony and kinship community. Without naval support, a campaign against Carthage was not feasible.

These failures are significant not because they define Cambyses as a ruler, but because they reveal something fundamental about the limits of empire. Even at the height of Persian power, geography, logistics, and the loyalties of subject peoples placed hard boundaries on what conquest could achieve. Cambyses had extended the empire to its natural limits in the northeast African theater. Pushing further required resources and cooperation that simply were not available.

The Crisis of Succession

While Cambyses was occupied in Egypt and its surroundings, the empire he had left behind began to fracture.

In 522 BCE, news reached him that a man claiming to be his brother Bardiya had seized the Persian throne. Whether this was the actual Bardiya - who Cambyses allegedly had killed years earlier - or an impostor, a Magian priest named Gaumata who had assumed Bardiya's identity, became one of the great disputed questions of ancient Persian history. The Behistun Inscription, Darius' own account, insists it was an impostor. Other interpretations suggest the rebellion may have been genuine, led by a Bardiya who had survived.

What is not disputed is the effect. The Persian heartland was in revolt. Cambyses began the journey back from Egypt to reclaim his throne.

He never arrived. Somewhere in Syria, in 522 BCE, Cambyses died. The cause of his death is uncertain - ancient sources offer varying accounts, including an accidental wound from his own sword. Whether his death was truly accidental, or whether something more deliberate occurred, cannot be determined from the surviving evidence.

The throne passed, after a period of violent struggle, to Darius I - a member of the Achaemenid royal family, but not a direct descendant of Cyrus. Darius would go on to reorganize the empire, codify its administration, and build Persepolis. His shadow has largely obscured Cambyses ever since.

What Cambyses Actually Built

Stepping back from the drama of his final months, Cambyses' reign deserves a more balanced accounting.

He inherited an empire and expanded it significantly. Egypt was not a minor acquisition - it was one of the ancient world's great civilizations, and bringing it under Persian control added enormous wealth, agricultural productivity, and symbolic prestige to the Achaemenid state. Persian control over Phoenicia and Egypt together gave the empire a dominant position in the eastern Mediterranean that would shape regional politics for generations.

His initial governance of Egypt showed pragmatic intelligence. By presenting himself as a legitimate pharaoh and respecting local religious structures - at least initially - he followed the same playbook that had made his father's conquests durable. The Achaemenid model of empire was not simply about military conquest; it was about integration, and Cambyses understood this.

His failures - the overextended campaigns into Kush and the Libyan desert - reflect the genuine difficulty of projecting power across extreme terrain with ancient logistics. They are not evidence of madness. They are evidence of ambition running up against the hard limits of the possible.

Key Takeaways

- Cambyses II ruled Persia from 529 to 522 BCE, succeeding his father Cyrus the Great and inheriting the largest empire in the world at that time.

- His conquest of Egypt in 525 BCE was a carefully planned campaign, building on groundwork Cyrus had laid, and was secured decisively at the Battle of Pelusium.

- Control of Phoenicia's naval forces was a critical strategic move that neutralized Egyptian sea power before the invasion began.

- Cambyses initially governed Egypt through conciliatory policies, adopting pharaonic titles and respecting local religious customs - a practice consistent with broader Achaemenid imperial strategy.

- Herodotus' portrayal of Cambyses as mad and impious is contradicted by contemporary Egyptian sources and archaeological evidence, and likely reflects later political and cultural biases.

- Planned expeditions against Kush, the Oasis of Amon, and Carthage largely failed due to logistical overreach and the limits of Persian power projection in North Africa.

- Cambyses died in 522 BCE under unclear circumstances while returning to Persia to suppress a rebellion, and was succeeded - after a period of conflict - by Darius I.

- His reign, though brief, permanently incorporated Egypt into the Persian Empire and demonstrated both the reach and the limits of Achaemenid power.

Cambyses II ruled for only seven years, but those years reshaped the map of the ancient world. Egypt, which had endured as an independent civilization for more than two thousand years, became a Persian satrapy. The eastern Mediterranean entered a new era of

Persian dominance that would last until Alexander the Great arrived two centuries later. What Cambyses built was real - even if the man himself has been buried under layers of hostile legend ever since. Who gets to write history, and whose version survives, is a question his story raises with unusual clarity - one that will follow the Persian Empire, and the empires that came after it, for as long as history is told.

Chapter 5
Darius I - Architect of Empire

The Persian Empire did not run itself. At its height, it stretched from the Aegean coast of modern Turkey to the banks of the Indus River in what is now Pakistan - a landmass so vast that a royal messenger riding hard could spend months crossing it. Holding that together required something more than conquest. It required administration.

Darius I understood this better than almost any ruler of the ancient world. When he came to power in 522 BCE, the empire Cyrus the Great had built was already enormous and already fragile. Darius spent the next thirty-six years turning a collection of conquered territories into something genuinely new: a functioning, integrated imperial state. He did not just rule the Persian Empire. He engineered it.

What follows traces Darius from his contested rise to power through the remarkable systems he built to govern millions of people across dozens of distinct cultures. It is a story about how empires actually work - not through brute force alone, but through roads, laws, languages, and the careful management of human loyalty.

A Throne Won by Cunning and Crisis

Darius did not inherit power in any straightforward sense. He seized it - and the story of how he did so tells us a great deal about the man he was.

When Cambyses II, son of Cyrus the Great, died in 522 BCE under circumstances that remain murky even today, the empire lurched into crisis. A man claiming to be Cambyses's brother Smerdis had already taken the throne, but Darius - a Persian nobleman of royal lineage, serving as a military officer - led a group of six other Persian nobles in a conspiracy to kill the pretender. Whether the man on the throne was truly Smerdis or an imposter, as Darius later claimed in his own inscriptions, is a question historians still debate. What is not debatable is the outcome: Darius emerged from the conspiracy as king.

What followed was not a smooth transition. Rebellions erupted across the empire almost immediately - in Babylon, in Media, in Egypt, in Persia itself. Within the first two years of his reign, Darius fought and won at least nineteen battles against nine different rebel leaders. He recorded all of this on a massive cliff face at Behistun, in what is now western Iran, carved in three languages for anyone who could read them. The Behistun Inscription is one of the most important documents from the ancient world. It reads partly like a military dispatch and partly like a very public argument that Darius was the rightful king, chosen by the god Ahura Mazda.

By 520 BCE, the rebellions were crushed. Darius had his throne. Now came the harder work.

Building the Machine: The Satrapy System

The Achaemenid Empire under Darius I, c. 500 BCE

The central challenge facing any ruler of the Achaemenid Empire was the same one that would trouble every large empire in history: how do you govern people who are thousands of miles away, speak different languages, worship different gods, and have their own deep traditions of law and custom?

Darius's answer was the satrapy - a provincial system that balanced central authority with local flexibility in ways that were genuinely sophisticated for the ancient world.

He reorganized the empire into approximately twenty provinces, each called a satrapy, each governed by an official called a satrap. The word itself comes from an Old Persian term meaning something like "protector of the realm." Satraps were powerful figures - they collected taxes, administered justice, maintained order, and commanded local military forces. In many ways, they functioned like regional kings.

But Darius was careful never to let them become kings in fact. He appointed satraps directly, choosing men he trusted - often relatives or members of the Persian nobility - rather than allowing local rulers to inherit the position automatically. He also installed two other officials alongside each satrap: a military commander and a financial secretary, both reporting independently to the royal court. No single man in any province held all the levers of power at once.

Then he sent inspectors. Known in Greek sources as "the king's eyes and ears," these royal officials traveled the empire unannounced, auditing accounts, investigating complaints, and reporting back to Darius. The satraps knew they were being watched. That knowledge mattered.

Some sources suggest the number of satrapies eventually grew to as many as thirty-six as the empire expanded and administrative needs became more complex. Whatever the precise count, the underlying logic remained consistent: divide the empire into manageable units, give local governors real authority, but never let that authority become independent.

The Roads That Held the Empire Together

An administrative system is only as good as its communications network. Darius grasped this with unusual clarity, and one of his most consequential achievements was the development of the Royal Road - a highway stretching roughly 2,700 kilometers from Susa, his administrative capital, to Sardis on the Aegean coast.

Susa became the nerve center of the empire after Darius established it as his administrative capital in 521 BCE. From there, royal couriers could carry messages along the Royal Road using a relay system of stations spaced at regular intervals - roughly a day's ride apart. A message that might take an ordinary traveler three months to carry could reach its destination in a matter of days.

This was not just impressive logistics. It was the physical infrastructure of imperial control. Darius could issue orders, receive reports, and respond to crises across an enormous distance with a speed that would have seemed remarkable to his subjects. The road also facilitated trade, tax collection, and the movement of armies - all the practical machinery of empire.

A Common Language for an Uncommon Empire

One of the quieter but more consequential decisions Darius made was the promotion of Imperial Aramaic as the standard administrative and legal language of the empire.

This was a pragmatic choice, not an ideological one. Aramaic was already widely spoken across the Near East as a trade and diplomatic language. By adopting it as the official tongue of imperial administration, Darius gave his bureaucracy a common medium of communication that could function across the empire's extraordinary linguistic diversity. A scribe in Babylon and a scribe in Egypt could correspond directly, without translation, using the same script and the same administrative vocabulary.

The decision reflected something important about how Darius thought about governance. He was not trying to erase local cultures or impose Persian identity on conquered peoples. He was trying to make the machinery of empire work. If Aramaic served that purpose better than Persian, then Aramaic it would be.

Law, Money, and the Logic of Integration

Darius applied the same pragmatic intelligence to law and economics.

Rather than imposing a single Persian legal code on all his subjects, he worked to harmonize existing regional legal traditions - Babylonian, Elamite, Egyptian - into a broader imperial framework. Local customs and laws were respected where they did not conflict with imperial authority. This approach reduced friction and made the empire easier to administer. People who felt their traditions were being respected were less likely to rebel.

On the economic side, Darius introduced a standardized system of weights and measures and promoted a common coinage - the gold daric - that facilitated trade across the empire. A merchant moving goods from the Indus Valley to the Mediterranean could operate within a recognizable economic framework throughout the journey. This kind of standardization, easy to overlook in a list of royal achievements, was genuinely transformative for commerce and taxation alike.

Tax collection itself was systematized. Each satrapy was assessed a fixed annual tribute based on its agricultural output and economic capacity. The Babylonians paid one amount; the Egyptians another; the Indian provinces another still. The assessments were not arbitrary - they reflected real calculations about what each region could bear. Darius wanted revenue, but he also understood that overtaxing a province was a reliable way to produce a rebellion.

Religious Tolerance as Imperial Policy

One of the most striking features of Darius's rule - and of the Achaemenid Empire more broadly - was its approach to religion. Darius himself was a devoted follower of Ahura Mazda, the supreme deity of Zoroastrianism, and his inscriptions invoke the god's favor repeatedly. But he did not require his subjects to share his faith.

Egyptian gods received royal support. Babylonian temples were maintained. Jewish communities in Babylon, displaced by earlier conquests, were permitted to practice their religion and eventually to return to their homeland. This was not sentimentality. Religious tolerance was imperial policy, and it worked. Peoples who could worship their own gods under Persian rule had one less reason to resist that rule.

The Limits of the System: Campaigns and Miscalculations

For all his administrative brilliance, Darius was not infallible. His military campaigns beyond the empire's established frontiers revealed the limits of ancient geographical knowledge - and the dangers of acting on incomplete information.

His expedition toward the Russian steppes, aimed at the nomadic Scythian peoples who lived north of the Black Sea, ended in retreat. The campaign was hampered by the vast, featureless terrain and by the Scythians' refusal to engage in the kind of pitched battle that Persian armies were designed to win. Without a fixed enemy to defeat or a city to capture, Darius's forces found themselves chasing shadows across unfamiliar ground. They withdrew without achieving their objectives.

The episode serves as a reminder that even the most sophisticated administrative system cannot compensate for flawed strategic assumptions. Darius's empire rested on an extraordinary foundation of practical intelligence - but that intelligence had its boundaries, and the steppes lay beyond them.

Key Figures and Turning Points

Darius I (522-486 BCE) stands as the central figure of this chapter, but understanding him requires understanding the context he operated in. He inherited an empire built by Cyrus the Great and expanded by Cambyses II, but he found it in crisis. His achievement was not conquest - it was consolidation. He transformed a collection of militarily subdued territories into a coherent administrative state.

Several moments defined his reign:

- **522-520 BCE**: The suppression of widespread rebellions following his seizure of power, documented in the Behistun Inscription - one of the most important primary sources from the ancient world.

- **521 BCE**: The establishment of Susa as the administrative capital, marking a deliberate shift toward systematic governance over military campaigning.

- Development of the Royal Road and the relay courier system, which gave the empire its nervous system.

- Promotion of Imperial Aramaic, which gave the empire its common language.

- Standardization of weights, measures, and coinage, which gave the empire its economic coherence.

Each of these was a choice, not an accident. Darius made them deliberately, and the empire he left behind when he died in 486 BCE was measurably more durable than the one he had inherited.

The Lasting Significance of Darius's Empire

What Darius built was not just a large kingdom. It was a model - one that later empires would study, consciously or not, for centuries.

The satrapy system anticipated the provincial governance structures of the Roman Empire. The use of a standardized administrative language prefigured similar decisions by later imperial powers from the Macedonians to the Ottomans. The principle of religious and cultural tolerance as a tool of imperial stability - rather than forced assimilation - would prove one of the most durable ideas in the history of governance.

Darius also demonstrated something easy to underestimate: that administration is itself a form of power. Armies can conquer territory, but they cannot hold it indefinitely without systems - systems of law, communication, taxation, and loyalty management. Darius understood this at a level that few rulers of his era matched.

His failures carry lessons as well. The Scythian campaign showed that even the best-organized empire cannot project power effectively into environments it does not understand. Geographic and cultural ignorance remained a persistent constraint on ancient imperial ambition, and Darius was not exempt from it.

Common Misconceptions

Research around Darius's reign surfaces several persistent misunderstandings worth addressing directly.

Darius was not the founder of the Persian Empire. That distinction belongs to Cyrus the Great, who established the Achaemenid Empire roughly a generation earlier. Darius's achievement was different - and in some ways more difficult. He inherited an empire in crisis and rebuilt it into something more durable.

The satrapy system was not simply a form of military occupation. Satraps were not garrison commanders. They were administrators with real governing responsibilities, operating within a carefully designed system of checks that prevented any single official from accumulating unchecked power.

Religious tolerance under Darius was not idealism. It was policy. Darius supported local religious traditions because doing so reduced resistance and made the empire easier to govern. The effect was genuinely tolerant, but the motivation was pragmatic.

The Behistun Inscription is not simply royal propaganda. While Darius certainly shaped his own narrative in the inscription, it also contains verifiable historical information and is one of the most important primary sources for understanding the early Achaemenid period. Scholars treat it critically, but they treat it seriously.

Darius's administrative innovations were not inevitable developments. They were choices, made by a specific person at a specific moment. The Persian Empire could have been governed very differently - and the fact that it was governed as well as it was reflects Darius's particular genius for institutional design.

Quick Summary

- Darius I ruled the Persian Empire from 522 to 486 BCE, coming to power through a conspiracy against a disputed claimant to the throne.

- He spent the first years of his reign suppressing widespread rebellions, documented in the famous Behistun Inscription carved in three languages.

- He reorganized the empire into approximately twenty satrapies, each governed by a satrap but checked by independently reporting military and financial officials.

- Royal inspectors - "the king's eyes and ears" - traveled the empire to audit satraps and report back to the court, preventing unchecked regional power.

- Darius established Susa as his administrative capital in 521 BCE and developed the Royal Road, a 2,700-kilometer highway enabling rapid communication across the empire.

- He promoted Imperial Aramaic as the standard administrative language, allowing bureaucrats across the empire's diverse regions to communicate in a common tongue.

- His legal reforms harmonized regional traditions - Babylonian, Elamite, Egyptian - into a broader imperial framework, reducing friction and respecting local customs.

- Standardized weights, measures, and the gold daric coinage unified the empire's economic systems and facilitated trade and taxation.

What Darius left behind in 486 BCE was not just an empire - it was a template. The systems he designed, the principles he applied, and even the mistakes he made would echo through the centuries that followed, shaping how later rulers thought about the problem of governing people they had never met, in places they would never visit, speaking languages they did not speak. That is the measure of genuine administrative genius: not that it solves every problem, but that it creates structures capable of outlasting the person who built them.

Chapter 6
Xerxes - War, Ambition, and Overreach

When Xerxes led his army across the Hellespont in 480 BC, he did something no Persian king had ever done before: he bridged two continents. His engineers lashed hundreds of boats together to form a floating causeway across the strait separating Asia from Europe, and his soldiers marched across it into a war that would define how the ancient world remembered him. For the Greeks, that crossing became a symbol of hubris - a king so drunk on power that he tried to chain the sea itself. But the story of Xerxes is far more complicated than the one the Greeks chose to tell.

The King Who Inherited an Unfinished War

Xerxes came to the Persian throne in 486 BC, inheriting an empire that stretched from Egypt to the borders of India - and a grudge that his father Darius had never settled. Ten years earlier, at the Battle of Marathon in 490 BC, a Persian expeditionary force had suffered a humiliating defeat at the hands of the Athenians. For the Achaemenid dynasty, which had built its legitimacy on the idea of an ever-expanding, divinely favored empire, that loss was not merely a military setback. It was an affront that demanded a response.

Darius had spent years planning a second invasion, but revolts in Egypt and Babylon consumed his attention, and he died before he could return to Greece. Xerxes inherited both the throne and the unfinished campaign. From the Persian perspective, the invasion of Greece was not an act of reckless ambition - it was the continuation of a strategic project, the logical extension of an empire that had been absorbing neighboring territories for generations.

What the Greeks experienced as an existential threat, the Persians understood as routine imperial consolidation. Greece was simply the next frontier.

The Scale of the Invasion

What Xerxes assembled for the 480 BC campaign was, by ancient standards, staggering. Greek sources describe an army of millions - figures almost certainly exaggerated for dramatic effect - but modern historians generally agree the force was enormous, likely numbering in the hundreds of thousands when combined land and naval contingents are considered. Dozens of subject peoples contributed troops: Medes, Lydians, Egyptians, Babylonians, Indians. The fleet alone reportedly numbered over a thousand ships.

This was not a raiding party. It was a statement.

Xerxes moved methodically. His engineers constructed those famous pontoon bridges across the Hellespont, and when a storm destroyed the first attempt, he reportedly ordered the sea itself to be whipped as punishment - a detail the Greeks recorded with gleeful horror, as proof of Persian arrogance. Whether or not the story is literally true, it captured something real about how the Greeks perceived their enemy: as a king who believed himself above nature, above limits, above the gods themselves.

That perception would shape everything that followed.

Thermopylae: The Pass That Became a Legend

In late summer of 480 BC, the Persian army reached the narrow coastal pass at Thermopylae, where a small Greek coalition force had positioned itself to slow the advance. For three days, roughly three hundred Spartans under King Leonidas - supported by several thousand allied Greek troops - held the pass against repeated Persian assaults.

From a purely military standpoint, the Greek defense at Thermopylae was tactically brilliant. The narrow terrain neutralized the Persian numerical advantage, forcing attackers into a bottleneck where discipline and heavy armor mattered more than sheer numbers. Persian casualties mounted. Elite units, including the famous Immortals, failed to break through.

Then a local Greek named Ephialtes showed the Persians a mountain path around the pass.

When Leonidas realized his position had been flanked, he dismissed most of the allied forces and remained with his Spartans - and a contingent of Thespians and Thebans - to fight a rearguard action that allowed the Greek army to retreat. Every last Spartan died. Leonidas died with them.

For the Greeks, Thermopylae became sacred ground almost immediately. The sacrifice of the three hundred was transformed into a moral parable about courage, duty, and the defense of freedom against tyranny. That story has echoed through Western culture ever since, from ancient epitaphs to modern films.

From the Persian side, Thermopylae was simply a tactical obstacle that had been overcome. The pass was cleared. The road to Athens lay open.

Salamis: Where the War Turned

Xerxes entered Athens in September of 480 BC and burned it. The Acropolis was torched, the temples destroyed. For the Persians, this was a symbolic and strategic victory - the city that had humiliated them at Marathon had been razed.

But Athens was not Greece. And the Athenian fleet was still intact.

What followed was the Battle of Salamis, fought in the narrow straits between the island of Salamis and the Attic coast. The Athenian commander Themistocles, who had spent years preparing for exactly this kind of confrontation, lured the Persian fleet into confined waters where its numerical superiority became a liability rather than an asset. Persian ships, many of them crewed by Phoenicians and Egyptians with varying degrees of loyalty to the empire, crowded together and fell into confusion. Greek triremes, lighter and more maneuverable, tore through them.

Xerxes watched the disaster unfold from a throne set up on the shore.

Salamis was not just a naval defeat. It was a strategic catastrophe. Without control of the sea, Xerxes could not reliably supply or reinforce his massive land army. He withdrew much of his force back to Asia, leaving a general named Mardonius to continue the campaign with a reduced army. The following year, at the Battle of Plataea in 479 BC, that army was defeated and Mardonius was killed. Persian forces never again attempted a major invasion of mainland Greece.

Reading the Defeat Honestly

Here is where the Greek narrative - compelling as it is - begins to obscure more than it reveals.

Thermopylae and Salamis were not the triumph of virtue over vice, of freedom over slavery, of small brave nations against a monstrous empire. They were military engagements shaped by terrain, logistics, leadership decisions, and a degree of Greek unity that was itself fragile and contested. Many Greek city-states had submitted to Persia without a fight. The Delphic Oracle had counseled accommodation. Even among those who resisted, cooperation was grudging and fractious.

Persian failure in Greece was, at its core, a failure of strategic overextension. Xerxes had committed an enormous force to a campaign at the far edge of his empire, across difficult terrain, dependent on a long and vulnerable supply chain. When the naval situation turned against him at Salamis, the entire operation became unsustainable. The Greeks did not defeat the Persian Empire - they defeated a Persian expedition. The empire itself remained intact, powerful, and dominant across the Near East for another century and a half.

Framing the Greek Wars as a story of moral destiny - civilization saved by courage - is satisfying. It is also selective history.

The King Behind the Campaign

Beyond the battlefield, Xerxes remains a figure whose complexity the Greek sources had little interest in preserving. Persian records reveal a capable administrator who continued the monumental building programs of his father. The great terrace at Persepolis, one of the ancient world's most spectacular architectural achievements, was substantially completed under his reign. Inscriptions from his court describe a king who understood himself as the chosen instrument of Ahura Mazda, the supreme deity of Zoroastrian faith, and who took his religious and administrative responsibilities seriously.

He also faced serious internal challenges. Revolts in Babylon and Egypt during the early years of his reign required military suppression. Court politics at Persepolis were treacherous - competing factions, powerful nobles, and ambitious relatives all jostled for influence. The later years of his reign were marked by growing instability within the court itself, and in 465 BC, Xerxes was assassinated in a palace conspiracy, killed by members of his own household.

The man who had bridged the Hellespont died not in battle, but in his own bedroom, betrayed by those closest to him.

Why Xerxes Still Matters

Xerxes has been poorly served by history - or rather, by whose history survived. The Greeks wrote voluminously about the wars; the Persians left administrative records, inscriptions, and architecture, but no narrative histories in the Greek tradition. As a result, the story of 480 BC has been told almost entirely from one side, filtered through the perspective of the victors, shaped by their need to make meaning from their unlikely survival.

Reframing Xerxes does not mean rehabilitating him or dismissing the genuine courage of those who resisted his invasion. It means recognizing that the Persian Wars were a collision between two complex civilizations, not a morality play. Xerxes was not a cartoon tyrant. He was a king managing the largest empire the world had yet seen, pursuing strategic objectives that made sense within his own imperial logic, and suffering a military reversal that - significant as it was - did not end his empire or his reign.

His story fills the gap between the confident expansion of Darius and the slow internal fractures that would eventually weaken the Achaemenid dynasty from within. The seeds of that decline were not planted at Salamis. They were planted in the court politics, the succession struggles, and the growing difficulty of holding together a vast, diverse empire through force of personality and divine mandate alone.

Key Takeaways

- Xerxes ascended to the Persian throne in 486 BC and inherited his father Darius's unfinished campaign against Greece.

- From the Persian perspective, the invasion of Greece was a continuation of imperial expansion, not an act of irrational aggression.

- At Thermopylae in 480 BC, a small Greek force delayed the Persian advance for three days before being outflanked; the Spartan last stand became one of history's most enduring military legends.

- At Salamis, the Greek fleet defeated the Persian navy in confined waters, making the Persian land campaign logistically unsustainable.

- Persian forces withdrew after the Battle of Plataea in 479 BC, but the Persian Empire itself remained powerful and intact.

- The Greek narrative of the wars emphasized moral and civilizational themes; the military reality was shaped more by terrain, logistics, and strategic overextension.

- Xerxes was also a builder and administrator; the great structures at Persepolis reflect the ambition and sophistication of his reign.

- He was assassinated in a palace conspiracy in 465 BC - a reminder that the greatest threats to Achaemenid power often came from within.

The Greek Wars did not break the Persian Empire, but they did reveal its limits. Xerxes had shown that even the mightiest force in the ancient world could be stopped when terrain, tactics, and determination aligned against it. What he could not have known was that the internal pressures building inside his court would prove more dangerous than any Greek spear. The empire he left behind was still vast, still formidable - but the cracks were beginning to show.

PART 3
HOW THE EMPIRE WORKED

Chapter 7
Governance and Administration

When Darius I seized the Persian throne in 522 BCE, he inherited an empire stretching from the Aegean coast to the edges of Central Asia - a territory so vast that no single ruler, however capable, could govern it alone. His solution was not to conquer more land. It was to build a machine.

What Darius constructed over the following decades became one of the ancient world's most sophisticated administrative systems - a framework of delegated authority, standardized law, and imperial communication that held together dozens of peoples, languages, and cultures under a single Persian crown. Understanding how that machine worked reveals something essential not just about the Achaemenid Empire, but about the very idea of organized power itself.

Three pillars supported Persian imperial governance: the satrapy system that distributed power across the empire's vast geography, the legal and social structures that maintained order within it, and the taxation apparatus that kept the whole enterprise funded and functional. Together, these systems made the Persian Empire not merely large, but durable - and their influence echoed long after the last Achaemenid king fell.

The Architecture of Empire: Satrapies

Cyrus the Great had laid the foundation. When he built the first Persian Empire, he established an early version of the satrapy system - regional provinces governed by appointed officials who answered to the king. It was a practical solution to an obvious problem: you cannot rule Babylon and Bactria from the same throne room.

But it was Darius I who transformed this rough framework into a genuine administrative architecture.

During his reign from 522 to 486 BCE, Darius expanded the number of satrapies to thirty-six, each one a distinct administrative unit with its own governor, its own local customs, and its own relationship to the imperial center. A satrapy was not simply a conquered territory. It was a managed one - a region integrated into the empire's economic and political life while retaining enough local character to remain governable.

The Satrap: Power at the Provincial Level

At the heart of each satrapy stood the satrap himself. The word comes from the Old Persian *xšaθrapāvan*, meaning "protector of the kingdom," and the role carried genuine weight. Satraps collected taxes, administered justice, maintained order, raised troops when required, and served as the king's representative within their territory.

Many satraps were members of the Persian nobility - often relatives of the king - which helped ensure loyalty and gave the crown a personal stake in each province's stability. But the position also carried real autonomy. A satrap governing a distant province like Egypt or Lydia operated with considerable independence simply because the king was too far away to micromanage every decision.

This created an inherent tension. Delegated power is efficient, but it is also dangerous. A satrap with enough resources, enough local support, and enough ambition could become a rival rather than a servant.

Checks on Satrapal Power

Darius understood this risk. To counterbalance satrapal authority, he built a system of oversight into the administrative structure itself. Military commanders within each satrapy reported directly to the king rather than to the local satrap, creating a parallel chain of command that prevented any single official from controlling both civil and military power simultaneously.

Royal secretaries and financial officers also operated within each province, sending independent reports back to the imperial court. And then there were the "eyes and ears of the king" - royal inspectors who traveled the empire, auditing accounts, investigating complaints, and reporting directly to Persepolis. No satrap could be entirely certain when one of these inspectors might arrive.

This layered oversight system was not foolproof. But it was thoughtful - a genuine attempt to balance the efficiency of local governance with the security of central control.

When the System Strained: The Great Satrap's Revolt

For roughly a century and a half, the satrapy system functioned with remarkable stability. Then, between 372 and 362 BCE, it cracked.

Under Artaxerxes II, a wave of satrapal rebellions swept across the western provinces in what historians call the Great Satrap's Revolt. Dissatisfaction with imperial policies - the precise grievances varied by region and figure - drove multiple governors to coordinate resistance against the crown. It was the most serious internal challenge the Achaemenid system had faced.

The revolt ultimately failed. Artaxerxes II managed to suppress the uprisings, in part because the rebel satraps never fully unified their efforts. But the episode exposed a structural vulnerability that had always lurked beneath the system's surface: when the center weakened, the periphery pulled away.

Alexander and the Satrapy's Survival

Perhaps the most striking testament to the satrapy system's effectiveness is what happened after the Achaemenid Empire fell. When Alexander the Great completed his conquest of Persia and stood over the body of Darius III - the last Achaemenid king - in 330

BCE, he faced the same administrative problem Cyrus had faced two centuries earlier. How do you govern an empire this large?

His answer was the same. Alexander kept the satrapy system largely intact, appointing his own governors to existing provincial structures rather than dismantling what he found. The machine was too useful to discard. Later, the Seleucid Empire that emerged from Alexander's fragmented conquests continued using satrapal-style governance, as did the Parthian Empire that followed, and the Sassanian Empire after that. A system designed in the sixth century BCE was still shaping administration in the seventh century CE.

Law and Order: Holding the Empire Together

An empire of thirty-six provinces and dozens of distinct peoples cannot function on military force alone. Soldiers can conquer territory; they cannot, by themselves, make it governable. For that, you need law - and a shared language in which to administer it.

Darius I understood this. His legal reforms were among the most consequential of his reign, and they operated on two levels simultaneously: the standardization of imperial communication and the codification of justice.

The Language of Empire

Across the Achaemenid Empire's vast territory, people spoke dozens of languages - Elamite, Babylonian, Egyptian, Greek, and many others. Darius did not try to eliminate this linguistic diversity. Instead, he promoted Imperial Aramaic as the administrative language of the empire.

Aramaic had already spread widely as a trade language across the Near East before the Persians arrived. By adopting it as the official medium for imperial correspondence, tax records, and legal documents, Darius gave his bureaucracy a common tongue without demanding that conquered peoples abandon their own. A scribe in

Egypt and a scribe in Anatolia could exchange official documents without a translator. That was not a small thing. It was the connective tissue of governance.

Justice Across Provinces

Persian imperial law operated alongside - rather than replacing - local legal traditions. This was a deliberate policy. Conquered peoples retained their customary laws and religious practices, which reduced resistance and made administration smoother. What the empire imposed was a framework of imperial authority on top of existing structures, not a wholesale replacement of them.

Satraps served as the primary judicial authorities within their provinces, hearing cases and dispensing justice in the king's name. For serious matters, or for disputes that crossed provincial boundaries, cases could be escalated toward the imperial center. The king himself stood as the ultimate legal authority - a living embodiment of justice whose decrees carried the force of divine sanction.

This system was not without its inequities. Persian nobles and imperial officials operated under different legal standards than ordinary subjects, and the king's justice could be arbitrary as well as fair. But as ancient imperial legal systems go, the Persian approach was notably pragmatic - focused on maintaining order and extracting compliance rather than imposing cultural uniformity.

The Role of Royal Roads

Law and order also depended on communication, and communication depended on infrastructure. Darius invested heavily in the Royal Road network - a system of maintained roads stretching across the empire, equipped with relay stations where royal messengers could exchange horses and continue riding without stopping.

A message could travel from Susa to Sardis - a distance of roughly 2,700 kilometers - in a matter of days rather than weeks. This was not just convenient. It was strategically essential. A king who could receive news quickly and dispatch orders faster than a rebellion could spread held a decisive advantage over any challenger.

Taxation: The Empire's Economic Engine

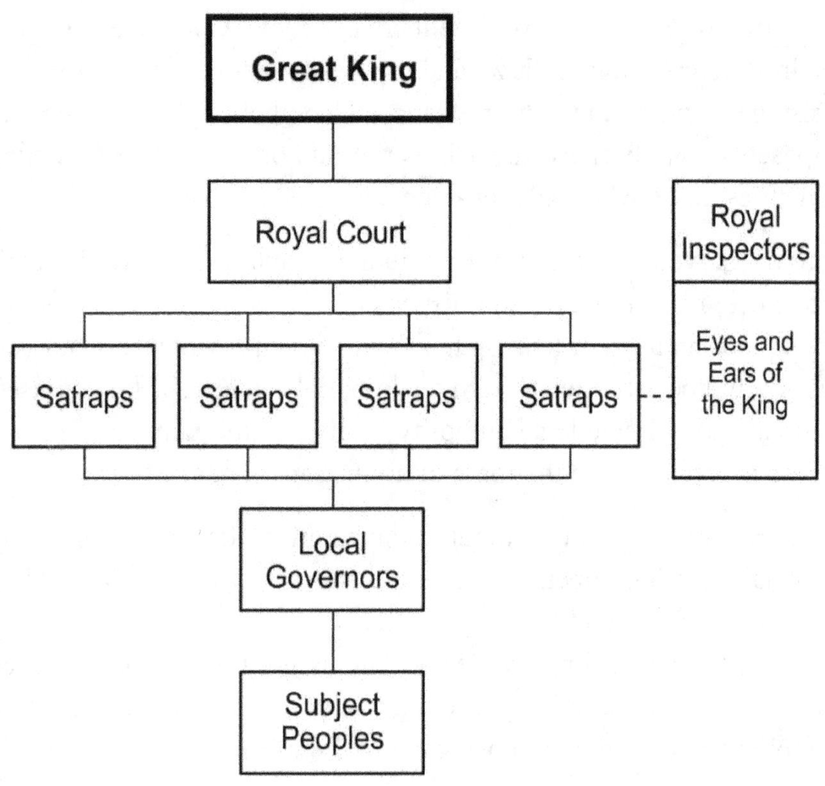

The Achaemenid power structure

Every army needs paying. Every road needs building. Every palace needs funding. Behind the administrative elegance of the satrapy system and the legal framework that held it together lay a more fundamental question: where did the money come from?

The answer was taxation - a system so carefully designed that it became one of the Persian Empire's most enduring legacies.

Darius and the Tribute System

Before Darius I, Persian taxation was relatively informal - a system of tribute payments that varied by region and lacked standardization. Darius changed this. As part of his broader administrative reforms, he established fixed tribute assessments for each satrapy, calculated according to the province's agricultural productivity, population, and resources.

Fixed assessments meant that satraps and their subjects knew in advance what was owed, reducing the scope for arbitrary extraction and making imperial revenue more predictable. The king could plan military campaigns and building projects with a clearer sense of what his treasury would contain.

Each satrapy paid its tribute in a combination of silver and goods - grain, livestock, textiles, and other commodities that the empire needed to function. The specific mix varied by region and by what each province could most efficiently produce. Egypt, with its extraordinary agricultural output, contributed heavily in grain. Provinces with access to silver mines paid in metal.

The Mechanics of Collection

Collecting tribute across an empire of this scale required its own bureaucratic infrastructure. Financial officers within each satrapy maintained records, oversaw assessments, and organized the physical transfer of wealth to imperial treasuries. The great treasury at Persepolis served as a central repository, but regional treasuries distributed the burden of storage and reduced the logistical challenge of moving vast quantities of goods across the empire.

Satraps themselves played a central role in tax collection, which was one reason the position was so powerful - and so potentially corrupting. A satrap who skimmed from the tribute flowing through his hands could enrich himself substantially before anyone in Persepolis noticed. This was another reason Darius maintained independent financial officers who reported directly to the crown: the temptation to exploit the system was simply too great to leave unchecked.

Beyond Tribute: Labor and Service

Taxation in the Persian Empire was not purely monetary. The empire also extracted value through labor obligations and military service. Conquered peoples could be required to provide workers for royal construction projects, soldiers for imperial armies, or specialized craftsmen for the great building programs at Persepolis and Susa.

This system of labor taxation was carefully managed. Records from Persepolis show that workers on royal construction projects received rations and, in some cases, wages, suggesting that the Persian approach to labor was more organized and less purely coercive than is sometimes assumed. The empire needed skilled workers, and it understood that starved or brutalized workers produced poor results.

The Long Shadow of Persian Fiscal Policy

When Alexander conquered the Achaemenid Empire, he found the treasuries at Persepolis and Susa filled with staggering quantities of accumulated wealth - the product of generations of systematic tribute collection. The scale of what he discovered reportedly astonished even his battle-hardened generals.

That wealth had not appeared by accident. It was the product of a fiscal system sophisticated enough to extract resources from dozens of provinces over centuries without triggering the kind of mass revolt that would have destroyed the empire's productive base. The Seleucid, Parthian, and Sassanian empires that followed all inherited and adapted Persian fiscal frameworks, recognizing that the system Darius had built was simply too effective to abandon.

Analysis: Why It Worked - and Why It Sometimes Didn't

What made the Persian administrative system so durable? Several factors stand out.

First, it was pragmatic rather than ideological. The Persians did not demand cultural conformity from conquered peoples. They demanded compliance - tribute, order, and acknowledgment of Persian sovereignty. Within those constraints, local customs, religions, and laws could continue largely undisturbed. This reduced the friction of conquest and made the empire easier to hold.

Second, the system built in redundancy. By separating military, civil, and financial authority within each satrapy, Darius ensured that no single official could accumulate enough power to threaten the center. The overlapping chains of command were sometimes inefficient, but they were also resilient.

Third, the investment in communication infrastructure - the Royal Roads, the relay stations, the standardization of Imperial Aramaic - meant that the empire could respond to crises faster than most of its rivals. Speed of information was a strategic asset, and Darius treated it as one.

But the system had limits. The Great Satrap's Revolt demonstrated that when the king was weak or distracted, the centrifugal forces built into a system of delegated authority could overwhelm the centripetal ones. The empire's sheer size meant that even the best-designed oversight mechanisms could not catch every abuse, every act of corruption, or every quietly building rebellion before it became serious.

The Persian administrative system was not perfect. Measured against the alternatives available in the ancient world, however, it was extraordinary - a genuine achievement of political engineering that shaped how empires were governed for nearly a millennium after Darius first put it in place.

Legacy and Long-Term Impact

The Achaemenid administrative model did not die with the empire. Alexander the Great's decision to preserve the satrapy system was not mere pragmatism - it was a recognition that the Persians had solved problems he had not yet figured out how to solve differently.

The Seleucid Empire, which controlled much of the former Persian territory from 312 to 63 BCE, operated satrapal-style governance as a matter of course. The Parthian Empire, which replaced Seleucid power and lasted from 247 BCE to 224 CE, maintained regional governors with broadly similar functions. And the Sassanian Empire, which ruled from 224 to 651 CE, drew explicitly on Achaemenid administrative traditions as part of its claim to be the legitimate heir of Persian imperial culture.

Each empire adapted what it inherited. But the core logic - delegate authority to regional governors, maintain central oversight, standardize communication, and extract revenue through systematic taxation - remained recognizable across all of them. The machine Darius built in the sixth century BCE was still running, in modified form, when Arab armies finally ended Sassanian rule in the seventh century CE.

Quick Summary

- Darius I expanded the satrapy system to thirty-six provinces, creating a framework for governing the empire's vast territory through appointed regional governors.

- Satraps held significant local authority but were counterbalanced by independent military commanders, financial officers, and royal inspectors who reported directly to the king.

- The Great Satrap's Revolt under Artaxerxes II revealed the system's vulnerability when central authority weakened, though the revolts ultimately failed.

- Alexander the Great preserved the satrapy system after conquering the Achaemenid Empire, recognizing its administrative effectiveness.

- Darius promoted Imperial Aramaic as the empire's administrative language, enabling communication across dozens of linguistically diverse provinces.

- Persian law allowed local legal traditions to continue under an imperial framework, reducing resistance and making governance more practical.

- Darius standardized tribute assessments by satrapy, creating predictable imperial revenue and reducing arbitrary extraction.

- The Persian administrative model - satrapies, standardized taxation, and layered oversight - influenced the Seleucid, Parthian, and Sassanian empires for nearly a thousand years.

What Darius built was more than an administrative system. It was a theory of power - one that recognized the limits of centralized control and found ways to work around them. The empires that followed, whether they knew it or not, were still working within the framework he had designed. That may be the most honest measure of any political achievement: not how long the empire itself lasted, but how long the ideas it produced continued to shape the world after it was gone.

Chapter 8
Roads, Trade, and Economy

Somewhere between Sardis and Susa, a royal courier was already riding.

He had fresh horses waiting at the next station, perhaps twenty miles ahead. The message he carried - sealed, official, urgent - would cross nearly 1,700 miles of mountains, rivers, and desert in roughly seven days. Not seven weeks. Seven days. In the fifth century BCE, that was not merely impressive. It was revolutionary.

The Achaemenid Persian Empire was, by any measure, the largest political entity the ancient world had yet produced. At its height under Darius I, it stretched from the Aegean coast of Anatolia in the west to the Indus Valley in the east, from the steppes of Central Asia in the north to the deserts of Egypt and Arabia in the south. Holding that together - administering it, taxing it, defending it, supplying it - required more than military power. It required infrastructure. It required logistics. It required, in a word, engineering.

What follows is an examination of the economic and physical architecture that made the Persian Empire function: the roads that carried messages and armies, the trade networks that moved goods across three continents, the tribute systems that funneled wealth toward the imperial center, and the markets and coinage that gave commerce its language. What emerges is a portrait of an empire that was not merely large, but sophisticated - one that understood, perhaps better than any state before it, that power flows along roads.

The Royal Road: Engineering an Empire

Darius I did not invent the road that bears his name. Older routes had existed across Anatolia and Mesopotamia for centuries before his reign. What Darius did - around 500 BCE - was something more consequential: he systematized, expanded, and institutionalized those routes into a single, coherent imperial highway.

At its full extent, the Royal Road ran approximately 1,677 miles, connecting the city of Sardis on the western edge of Anatolia to Susa, one of the Achaemenid capitals in the heart of Persia. Along the way, it passed through some of the ancient world's most varied terrain - the fertile plains of Mesopotamia, the mountain passes of the Zagros range, the river crossings of the Tigris and Euphrates. Building and maintaining a road across all of that was an enormous undertaking, requiring sustained imperial investment and a workforce drawn from the empire's many subject peoples.

What made the Royal Road more than just a path was its infrastructure. At regular intervals - roughly every fifteen to twenty miles, approximately the distance a horse could travel at speed before tiring - Darius established a chain of relay stations. Each station kept fresh horses and riders ready at all times. A message handed off at one station would be picked up by a new courier at the next, then the next, in an unbroken chain that could carry official communications from one end of the empire to the other in a matter of days.

The Greek historian Herodotus, writing in the fifth century BCE, described the system with undisguised admiration. "Neither snow, nor rain, nor heat, nor darkness of night prevents these couriers from completing their designated stages with utmost speed," he wrote - a passage so enduring that a version of it was later inscribed on the main post office in New York City, more than two thousand years after the empire that inspired it had fallen.

Speed as a Tool of Power

To appreciate what the Royal Road meant for the Achaemenid Empire, consider the problem it solved.

An empire spanning three million square miles cannot be governed by slow communication. A rebellion in Lydia, a flood in Babylon, a border incursion in the east - all of these demanded responses that were timely enough to matter. Without fast, reliable communication, a Persian king sitting in Susa or Persepolis was effectively blind to events happening hundreds of miles away. By the time a conventional messenger arrived with news, the crisis might already have spiraled beyond control.

The relay system changed that calculus entirely. Royal decrees, military orders, tax assessments, and administrative reports could now travel at a speed that kept the imperial center genuinely connected to its periphery. Governors in distant satrapies knew that their decisions were visible to Persepolis. Local administrators understood that the king's instructions could arrive within days, not months.

That knowledge alone - the awareness of being watched, of being reachable - was a form of control.

The road also served military purposes. Armies could move along it more efficiently than through open terrain, and the same relay stations that carried messages could supply and support troop movements. When Darius needed to project force toward the western frontier or respond to unrest in Egypt, the Royal Road was the mechanism by which Persian military power traveled.

A Network, Not Just a Road

THE PERSIAN EMPIRE, CIRCA 500 BCE

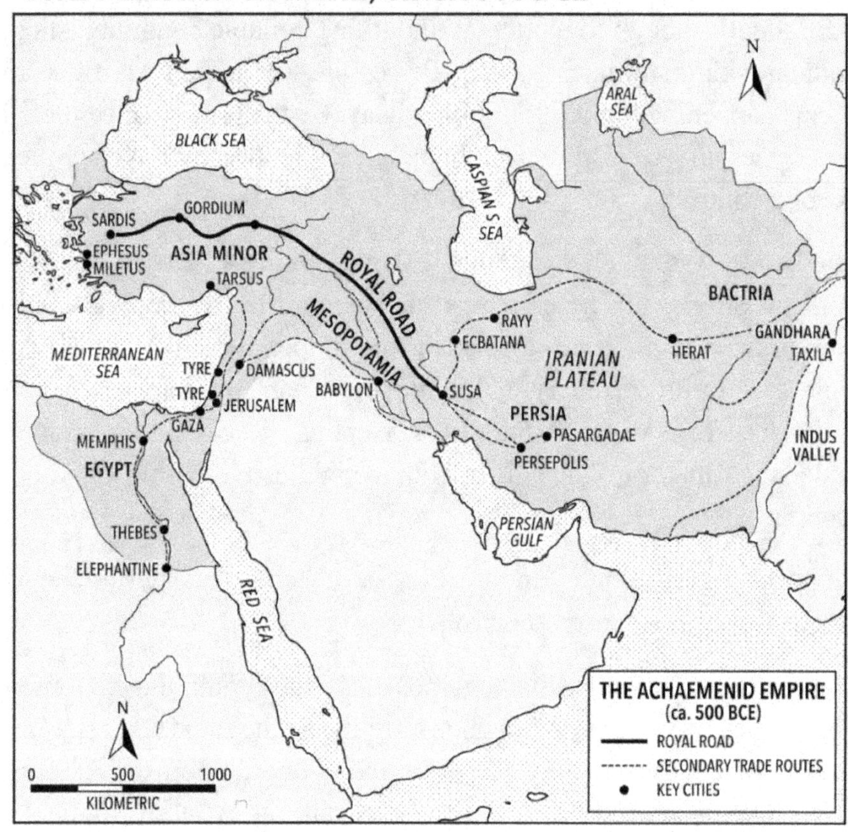

The Royal Road and major trade routes, c. 500 BCE

It would be a mistake to imagine the Royal Road as a single isolated highway cutting through empty land. It was the spine of a much larger network.

Branching routes connected the main road to provincial capitals, ports, and frontier outposts. Trade paths that had existed for generations were absorbed into the imperial system, given stations, guards, and official recognition. The result was something closer to a web than a line - a system of connected routes that made the Achaemenid Empire genuinely accessible for merchants, officials, soldiers, and diplomats alike.

This network had consequences that extended far beyond administrative convenience. It created the physical conditions for long-distance trade on a scale the ancient Near East had not previously seen. Goods moving along the Royal Road and its branches could travel from the Mediterranean coast to the Persian Gulf, from Egypt to the Indus Valley, with a degree of security and predictability that made commerce viable across enormous distances.

Merchants moving through the empire encountered a world that, at least in principle, was organized for movement. Caravanserais - rest stops for traveling merchants and their animals - dotted the major routes. Imperial guards provided a measure of security against banditry. The same relay infrastructure that served royal couriers also made it possible for private traders to move goods with greater confidence.

Trade Across Three Continents

The Achaemenid Empire sat at the center of the ancient world's most important trade corridors. To its west lay the Mediterranean and the commercial networks of Greece, Phoenicia, and Egypt. To its east lay the routes that would eventually be formalized as the Silk Road, connecting Central Asia to India and beyond. To its south lay the Persian Gulf and the maritime trade routes linking Mesopotamia to Arabia and East Africa.

Controlling this geography meant that Persia was not merely a participant in ancient trade. It was, in many respects, the hub through which much of that trade flowed.

Goods moving through the empire were extraordinarily diverse. Textiles, metals, spices, grain, timber, horses, and luxury goods of every description traveled along Persian roads and waterways. Lapis lazuli from Afghanistan moved westward toward Egypt and the

Mediterranean. Grain from the fertile plains of Mesopotamia fed populations across the empire. Timber from Lebanon supplied construction projects in Persepolis and Susa. Egyptian grain, Lydian silver, Indian spices - the empire's trade networks functioned as a mechanism for redistributing the natural wealth of an enormous and geographically varied territory.

This commerce was not incidental to Persian power. It was part of how the empire sustained itself. A prosperous merchant class meant taxable commerce. Busy trade routes meant well-maintained roads. The movement of goods across the empire reinforced the same networks that carried royal messages and military supplies. Commerce and control, in the Achaemenid system, were deeply intertwined.

Tribute, Taxation, and the Flow of Wealth

If trade represented the voluntary movement of goods, tribute represented the compulsory one. And in the Achaemenid Empire, tribute was the financial bedrock on which everything else rested.

Darius I reorganized the empire's fiscal system with characteristic thoroughness. He divided the empire into roughly twenty administrative provinces, known as satrapies, each governed by a satrap - typically a Persian nobleman, often a member of the royal family. Each satrapy was assessed a fixed annual tribute, payable in silver or in kind, calculated according to the province's estimated agricultural and commercial productivity.

The amounts involved were staggering. Ancient sources record tribute figures that, even accounting for the difficulty of translating ancient monetary values into modern terms, suggest an imperial revenue stream of extraordinary scale. Egypt alone was assessed at 700 talents of silver annually. Babylon contributed 1,000 talents. The total annual tribute flowing into the Achaemenid treasury from all satrapies combined was, by ancient accounts, in the range of several thousand talents of silver - a sum that dwarfed the revenues of any contemporary state.

This wealth did not simply accumulate in royal treasuries, though vast amounts of silver and gold were indeed stored at Persepolis and Susa. It was also redistributed. The empire spent lavishly on construction - the great palaces at Persepolis, the road network itself, irrigation projects, and harbor works. It paid its armies, its administrators, and the vast workforce of craftsmen, laborers, and specialists who kept the imperial machine running. Royal gifts to loyal nobles and subject kings were another channel through which imperial wealth circulated back into the economy.

Coinage and the Language of Commerce

One of the most significant economic innovations of the Achaemenid period was the formalization of coinage as a tool of imperial commerce and administration.

The Persians did not invent coinage - that credit belongs to the Lydians of western Anatolia, whose kingdom Cyrus the Great conquered in the mid-sixth century BCE. But the Achaemenids adopted and adapted the Lydian innovation with considerable sophistication. Under Darius I, the empire introduced the gold daric, a coin bearing the image of the king as an archer, which became one of the most widely recognized and trusted currencies in the ancient world.

The daric was a high-value coin, used primarily for large transactions, royal payments, and international trade. Alongside it circulated the silver siglos, a smaller denomination more suited to everyday commerce. Together, these coins gave merchants and administrators a standardized medium of exchange that worked across the empire's many languages, cultures, and local economies.

Before standardized coinage, long-distance trade required constant negotiation over the weight and purity of metal payments - a cumbersome process that added friction and risk to every transaction. A trusted imperial coin removed much of that friction. A merchant in Sardis and a merchant in Babylon could both accept a daric with confidence, knowing its weight and gold content had been guaranteed by the Persian crown.

Coinage also served political purposes. Every daric that changed hands carried the image of the Persian king - a subtle but persistent reminder of whose empire one was trading within. Money, in the Achaemenid system, was not merely economic. It was a statement of sovereignty.

Markets, Merchants, and the Imperial Economy

Beyond the grand mechanisms of tribute and coinage, the Persian economy was animated by the ordinary activity of markets - local, regional, and long-distance.

Major cities within the empire - Babylon, Memphis, Sardis, Susa - were commercial centers of the first order, home to merchants, artisans, bankers, and traders from across the known world. Babylon in particular retained its status as one of the ancient world's great commercial hubs long after its incorporation into the Achaemenid Empire. Its markets handled grain, textiles, metals, and financial instruments of surprising complexity, including contracts, loans, and receipts that archaeologists have recovered in large numbers from cuneiform clay tablets.

Merchants operating within the empire were not exclusively Persian. Phoenician traders, Greek merchants, Aramaic-speaking middlemen, and Indian traders all moved goods through Achaemenid territory. The empire's relative tolerance of diverse peoples and practices - a defining feature of Achaemenid governance - extended to commerce. Foreign merchants were generally permitted to trade, own property, and conduct business under the protection of Persian law.

This cosmopolitan commercial environment was one of the empire's genuine strengths. By drawing in merchants and traders from across the ancient world, the Achaemenid economy benefited from networks, knowledge, and goods that no purely Persian enterprise could have generated on its own.

Infrastructure That Outlasted the Empire

When Alexander the Great conquered the Achaemenid Empire between 334 and 323 BCE, he inherited not just its territory and its treasury, but its infrastructure. The Royal Road did not disappear with the fall of Persepolis. The Seleucid kings who ruled much of the former Persian Empire after Alexander's death maintained and extended the road network. The Parthians who followed them did the same. Even Rome, building its own legendary road system centuries later, was working within a tradition of imperial infrastructure that the Achaemenids had helped establish.

The influence was not merely physical. The idea that a great empire required fast communication, standardized currency, and organized trade routes - that these were not luxuries but necessities of governance - was a lesson the Persian Empire had demonstrated at scale. Later empires learned it, in part, by observing what Persia had built.

The daric, too, left its mark. Persian gold coins circulated in the Mediterranean world long after the empire's fall, trusted precisely because of the reputation for quality and consistency that Darius's minting standards had established. In the ancient economy, trust was hard to build and easy to lose. The Achaemenids built it, and it outlasted them.

Quick Summary

- Around 500 BCE, Darius I systematized the Royal Road, a 1,677-mile highway connecting Sardis in Anatolia to Susa in Persia, complete with relay stations every fifteen to twenty miles.

- The road's courier relay system could carry royal messages across the empire in approximately seven days, giving the Persian king genuine, real-time administrative reach over his vast territory.

- Trade networks under the Achaemenids connected the Mediterranean, Central Asia, the Indian subcontinent, and East Africa, with Persia functioning as the geographic and commercial hub of the ancient world.

- Darius reorganized the empire's tribute system, dividing it into roughly twenty satrapies each assessed a fixed annual payment, generating revenues that dwarfed those of any contemporary state.

- The gold daric and silver siglos - standardized imperial coins introduced under Darius - gave merchants across the empire a trusted medium of exchange and served as a daily reminder of Persian sovereignty.

- Major cities like Babylon and Sardis functioned as cosmopolitan commercial centers, drawing merchants from across the known world and handling financial instruments of considerable sophistication.

- The Royal Road and the broader infrastructure of Achaemenid commerce influenced the Seleucids, Parthians, and Romans, demonstrating that the empire's economic legacy outlasted its political one by centuries.

Roads are easy to take for granted. They are, after all, just paths - dirt and stone, worn smooth by feet and hooves and wheels. But the Royal

Road was never just a path. It was an argument, made in infrastructure, that an empire stretching from Egypt to India could be held together not only by force, but by connection - by the daily movement of messages, goods, and people along routes that the Persian crown had built, maintained, and protected. That argument proved persuasive enough that the empires which followed Persia kept making it, in their own languages and their own stone, for centuries to come.

Chapter 9
Art, Architecture, and Language

Stand at the eastern staircase of Persepolis on a clear morning, and you feel it immediately - the weight of intention. Every carved figure, every column base, every precisely cut stone block speaks not of accident but of design. This was a place built to make a point.

The Achaemenid Persian Empire, which stretched from the Aegean coast to the borders of India at its height, is often remembered as a military and administrative colossus - the great adversary of Greece, the empire that Cyrus built and Alexander burned. But to understand Persia only through its armies and satrapies is to miss what made it genuinely extraordinary. The Achaemenids were not merely conquerors. They were builders, patrons, and communicators who used stone, image, and language with extraordinary deliberateness. Their art was not decoration. Their architecture was not vanity. Both were instruments of a coherent imperial vision, one that sought to project power, legitimacy, and divine favor across a world of staggering cultural diversity.

What follows turns from the battlefield and the administrative hall to the carved relief, the inscribed column, and the written word. It asks what Achaemenid art, architecture, and language actually tell us about how this empire understood itself - and how it wanted the world to understand it.

Writing an Empire: Old Persian and the Languages of Power

Language is never politically neutral. Every empire chooses how it speaks, and that choice reveals something essential about how it governs.

The Achaemenids operated in a multilingual world, and they knew it. Their empire encompassed dozens of peoples who spoke Elamite, Aramaic, Babylonian, Egyptian, Greek, and many other tongues. Rather than imposing a single administrative language by force, the Persians made a pragmatic and revealing choice: they used Elamite as the primary language of imperial administration.

Elamite was the ancient language of the region centered on Susa, one of the empire's great capitals. It was not the native tongue of the Persian kings, but it was the language of the scribes and accountants who kept the empire running. The thousands of clay tablets discovered at Persepolis - known as the Persepolis Fortification Tablets - are written overwhelmingly in Elamite, recording rations of grain, wine, and livestock distributed to workers, officials, and travelers across the imperial heartland. These are not grand documents. They are receipts. But they reveal an empire that ran on organized, literate bureaucracy, and that trusted Elamite-speaking administrators to keep the machinery turning.

Old Persian was a different matter entirely. This was the language of kings - the tongue in which the Achaemenid monarchs addressed posterity, the gods, and themselves. Old Persian was written in a cuneiform script that appears to have been developed specifically for royal use, likely under Darius I, who reigned from 522 to 486 BC. It was not a language of commerce or administration. It was a language of proclamation.

Royal inscriptions in Old Persian appear across the empire - carved into cliff faces, stamped onto foundation tablets, chiseled into palace walls. Many of the most significant come from Susa and from Naqsh-e Rostam, the great rock-cut necropolis near Persepolis where Darius and his successors were buried. Scholars have continued to re-examine these inscriptions over the centuries, and corrections to previously misread or missing texts have repeatedly refined our understanding of both the language itself and the ideology it expressed.

One concept that emerges repeatedly from these inscriptions is the Old Persian word *farnah-* - a term denoting royal splendor, divine grace, and the luminous quality of legitimate kingship. It appears in royal epithets and personal names across the empire, including the Greek rendering Φαρνάουας. This was not mere flattery. *Farnah-* represented a theological claim: that the king ruled because the gods - above all, Ahura Mazda - had chosen him and endowed him with a visible, almost radiant authority. To carve that word into stone was to inscribe divine mandate into the very rock of the empire.

The Grammar of Stone: Persepolis and Imperial Iconography

Darius I founded Persepolis - known in Old Persian as *Parsa* - around 518 BC, and construction continued under his son Xerxes and later kings. Situated on a vast artificial terrace in the Marvdasht plain of modern-day Iran, Persepolis was not a commercial city or a military fortress. It was a ceremonial capital, a stage on which the empire performed its own greatness.

What survives today - even after Alexander the Great's forces burned and looted the site in 330 BC - remains breathtaking. Massive stone staircases lead up to columned halls. Doorways are framed by colossal guardian figures, part human and part bull. And covering the walls and stairways in extraordinary detail are the reliefs: hundreds of carved figures marching in procession, carrying gifts, leading animals, and standing in attendance before the king.

These reliefs are among the most studied and most revealing artifacts of the ancient world. They are not narrative scenes in the way that Egyptian or Assyrian reliefs often are - there are no battles depicted, no enemies crushed underfoot, no triumphant slaughter. Instead, the Persepolis reliefs show order. Harmony. Submission rendered as gift-giving.

The most famous sequence is the Apadana staircase relief, which depicts delegations from across the empire - scholars have identified representations of peoples from Lydians to Ethiopians, from Indians to Scythians - each bringing tribute appropriate to their homeland. One group leads horses. Another carries vessels. A third brings folded textiles. Every delegation is shown in respectful procession, moving toward the king.

This was ideology in stone. The message was unmistakable: the world comes to Persia. Diversity is real, but it is organized. Every people has its place in the imperial order, and that order flows from the king.

What makes the Persepolis reliefs particularly striking is their tone. Unlike the brutal triumphalism of Assyrian palace art - where enemies are shown impaled, beheaded, or fleeing in terror - the Achaemenid reliefs present a vision of dignified inclusion. The tribute-bearers are not humiliated. They walk upright, their clothing and physical features rendered with care and specificity. The empire, the imagery insists, is not a machine of domination. It is a harmonious community of peoples, each recognized, each contributing, all united under Persian rule.

Whether that vision matched the lived reality of imperial subjects is another question entirely. But as a statement of how the Achaemenids wished to be seen - and how they wished to see themselves - it is remarkably coherent.

Architecture as Ideology

Persepolis was not built to be lived in. It was built to be experienced.

The approach to the site was carefully choreographed. Visitors - whether foreign ambassadors, subject kings, or Persian nobles - climbed a broad ceremonial staircase wide enough, ancient sources suggest, for horses to ascend. They passed through the Gate of All Nations, a massive structure flanked by guardian bulls, before entering the terrace proper. Every step of the journey was designed to communicate scale, order, and the overwhelming authority of the Persian king.

Darius I understood architecture the way a modern political strategist understands media. His building projects were not simply expressions of wealth. They were arguments. The sheer scale of Persepolis - its columns rising to heights of twenty meters, its terrace covering an area of roughly 125,000 square meters - was itself a claim about the nature of Persian power. Only a king blessed by Ahura Mazda, ruling over a world of obedient peoples, could command such a construction.

And yet Persepolis was also a synthesis. Scholars have long noted the extraordinary diversity of artistic and architectural influences visible in the site's construction. Egyptian-style cavetto cornices appear alongside Mesopotamian-style glazed brick. Greek Ionic column bases stand near Persian-style bull capitals. The workforce that built Persepolis, as the Fortification Tablets confirm, included skilled craftsmen from across the empire - Egyptians, Babylonians, Lydians, Ionians - working alongside Persian laborers.

This was not cultural confusion. It was a deliberate statement. By incorporating the artistic traditions of subject peoples into the fabric of the imperial capital, the Achaemenids were making a visual argument: all roads lead here. All cultures contribute to Persian greatness. The empire does not erase what it absorbs - it elevates it.

Susa, the administrative capital, offered a parallel case. Darius's palace there was built with materials and craftsmen drawn from across the empire, and a foundation inscription he left behind lists them explicitly - cedar from Lebanon, gold from Sardis and Bactria, lapis lazuli from Sogdiana, silver and ebony from Egypt. The inscription reads almost like a catalogue of imperial reach. Every material was a trophy, and the building itself was a map of the empire's extent.

Reading the Reliefs: What the Carvings Actually Tell Us

Scholarship on Achaemenid art has evolved considerably since European travelers first began documenting Persepolis in the seventeenth century, following references in classical and biblical texts that pointed toward the site's existence. Early interpretations often filtered the reliefs through Greek or biblical frameworks - seeing Persian art as derivative, or as merely the backdrop to stories told by Herodotus and the Book of Esther.

More recent scholarship has worked to read the reliefs on their own terms, and the results have been revealing. The identification of specific delegations in the Apadana procession, for instance, has been refined through careful comparison with textual sources and with the physical features, clothing, and tribute objects depicted. Each delegation is distinct, and the distinctions were intentional - the artists were not producing generic "foreigners" but specific peoples, recognizable to those who knew them.

Re-examinations of inscriptions from Susa and Naqsh-e Rostam have also yielded important corrections to earlier readings. Some texts had been misread due to damage or the difficulty of the script; others contained gaps that were filled speculatively by early scholars. Updated readings have sharpened our understanding of royal titulature, of the theological claims embedded in official language, and of the relationship between Old Persian and Elamite in the imperial context.

What emerges from this ongoing scholarly work is a picture of an empire that was deeply self-aware about its own representation. The Achaemenids were not passive subjects of history. They were active shapers of their own image, and they brought to that task the same organizational intelligence they brought to taxation and military logistics.

Legacy and Long-Term Impact

Recognition of Achaemenid sites began in earnest in the seventeenth century, when European travelers connected classical and biblical references to ruins on the Iranian plateau. But serious archaeological and epigraphic work came much later, and the interpretation of Achaemenid art and language has continued to develop into the present day.

What that long process of discovery has revealed is a civilization of genuine cultural sophistication. Persia was not, as some ancient Greek sources implied, a despotic monolith crushing diversity underfoot. Its art celebrated diversity - carefully, selectively, and always in service of imperial ideology, but celebrated nonetheless. Its language policy was pragmatic and multilingual. Its architecture synthesized traditions from across the known world into something distinctly and powerfully Persian.

Alexander's burning of Persepolis in 330 BC - whether deliberate policy or drunken accident, as ancient sources debate - destroyed one of the ancient world's great cultural monuments. But it did not erase what the site had meant. The reliefs that survived, the tablets that lay buried for millennia, and the inscriptions carved into cliff faces across Iran have continued to speak. They speak of an empire that understood, with unusual clarity, that power is not only exercised through force. It is also communicated through beauty, through language, and through the stories a civilization chooses to tell about itself in stone.

Quick Summary

- The Achaemenid Empire (550-330 BC) used art, architecture, and language as deliberate instruments of imperial ideology, not merely as cultural expressions.

- Elamite served as the primary administrative language, while Old Persian was reserved for royal proclamations and monumental inscriptions.

- Old Persian was likely developed as a written script under Darius I, and key inscriptions at Susa and Naqsh-e Rostam remain central to understanding Achaemenid royal ideology.

- The concept of *farnah-* - divine royal splendor - appears repeatedly in inscriptions and names, encoding a theological claim about the king's legitimacy directly into official language.

- Persepolis, founded by Darius I around 518 BC and expanded by Xerxes, was a ceremonial capital designed to stage imperial power through architecture, scale, and visual symbolism.

- The Apadana staircase reliefs depict tribute-bearing delegations from across the empire in a tone of dignified order - a sharp contrast to the triumphalist violence of Assyrian palace art.

- Achaemenid architecture deliberately incorporated artistic traditions from Egypt, Mesopotamia, Greece, and Persia itself as a visual argument for the empire's synthesizing power.

- Ongoing scholarly re-examination of Achaemenid inscriptions and reliefs continues to refine earlier interpretations, deepening our understanding of Persian imperial culture.

What the Achaemenids built at Persepolis was not simply a palace complex. It was a theory of empire made visible - an argument, carved in stone and painted in color, that Persian rule was not conquest but order, not domination but harmony. That argument was always, at least in part, a fiction. But it was a remarkably sophisticated one, and the civilization capable of producing it deserves to be understood on its own terms.

PART 4
LIFE INSIDE ANCIENT PERSIA

Chapter 10
Court Life and Royal Power

Imagine standing at the foot of a staircase carved from pale limestone, each step broad enough to accommodate a horse and rider moving side by side. Above you, the stone is alive with figures - tribute-bearers from across a continent, each delegation rendered in precise detail, each wearing the distinctive dress of their homeland. Armenians lead a horse. Lydians carry golden vessels. Ethiopians offer an okapi. And at the top of this processional ascent, somewhere beyond the columns that rise twenty meters into the open Persian sky, waits the king.

This was Persepolis - not a city in any ordinary sense, but a stage. A place engineered to make power visible, to translate the abstract fact of empire into something a human body could feel in its bones.

A Stage Built for Kings

The Achaemenid Empire stretched from the Aegean coast to the Indus Valley between roughly 550 and 330 BCE - the largest political entity the ancient world had yet produced. Governing it required more than armies and administrators. It required a shared language of authority: symbols, rituals, and spaces that communicated, without ambiguity, who stood at the center of the world.

Persepolis was that language made stone.

Construction began under Darius I, who came to power in 522 BCE and immediately set about transforming a rocky terrace in the Zagros foothills into something unprecedented. He did not build a capital in the conventional sense. Persepolis was not a commercial hub or a military headquarters. It was a ceremonial complex, a place where the empire's meaning was performed rather than administered. His successor Xerxes continued the work, adding halls, gateways, and apartments that expanded both the physical footprint and the symbolic ambition of the site.

What they created together was a place where the act of appearing before the king became, itself, a political event.

The Architecture of Awe

At the heart of Persepolis stood the Apadana - the great audience hall commissioned by Darius I. Even in ruin, its scale stops visitors cold. At its peak, the hall was supported by thirty-six columns, each standing roughly twenty meters tall and topped with distinctive double-headed animal capitals: bulls, lions, and eagles carved with extraordinary precision. The roof they supported would have covered an area large enough to hold thousands of people.

But the Apadana was not simply large. It was designed to overwhelm.

Approaching the hall meant ascending the famous processional staircases, whose carved reliefs depicted delegations from across the empire - twenty-three distinct peoples, scholars have counted, each group identifiable by costume, hairstyle, and the specific tribute they carried. Medes in rounded caps. Elamites with a lioness and cubs. Indians with jars and a donkey. Scythians with horses and folded trousers. The visual effect was deliberate and cumulative: by the time a visitor reached the king's presence, they had already walked through a carved map of his dominion.

This was architecture as argument. Every column, every relief, every carefully proportioned doorway said the same thing: the world is vast, and it belongs to one man.

Susa: The Empire's Administrative Heart

If Persepolis was the empire's ceremonial soul, Susa was its working mind. One of the oldest cities in the ancient world - inhabited for thousands of years before the Achaemenids arrived - Susa served as a primary administrative capital, the place where the machinery of empire actually ran.

Darius I rebuilt and expanded Susa's royal palace on a grand scale, and the palace's own inscriptions record his pride in what he had accomplished. He noted, with evident satisfaction, that the materials and craftsmen came from across the empire: cedar from Lebanon, gold from Sardis and Bactria, ivory from Ethiopia and India, stone-cutters from Ionia and Sardis. The palace at Susa was, in this sense, a physical embodiment of the same multicultural logic that animated Persepolis - the empire's diversity displayed as a form of royal achievement.

Susa's position also made it practical. Located in what is now southwestern Iran, it sat at the intersection of major trade and communication routes, making it a natural hub for the satrapies - the provincial governorships - that administered Achaemenid territory. Royal correspondence flowed through Susa. Tax records were compiled there. The famous Royal Road, which connected the western reaches of the empire to the Persian heartland, had one of its termini at Susa's gates.

The two cities served complementary purposes. Susa governed. Persepolis performed.

The Rituals of Royal Presence

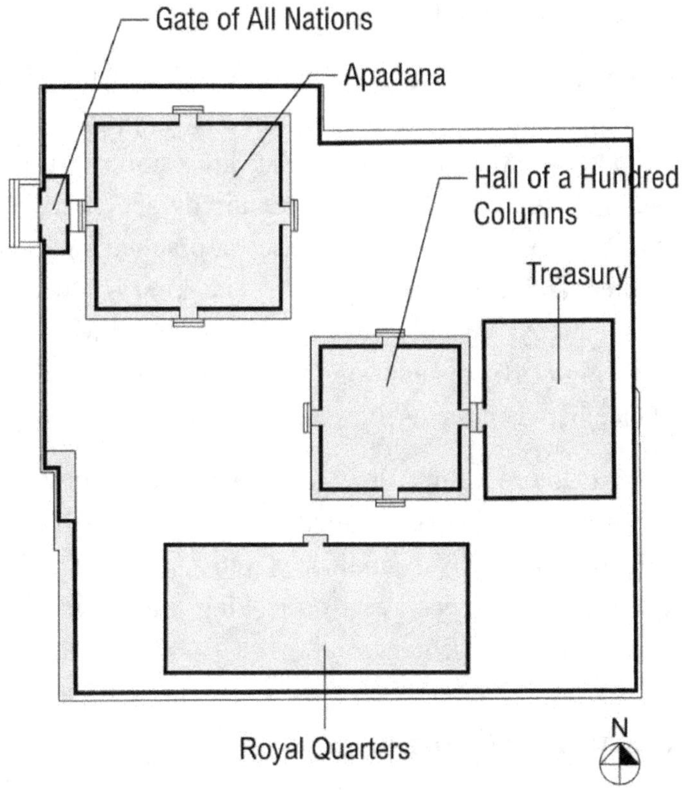

Persepolis - key structures of the ceremonial capital

What actually happened at Persepolis during its great ceremonial occasions? Evidence suggests that the most important was the Nowruz celebration - the Persian New Year, which fell at the spring equinox. This was the moment when delegations from across the empire converged on the terrace to present tribute to the king, and the reliefs on the Apadana staircase almost certainly depict exactly this event, frozen in stone for eternity.

The logistics alone were staggering. Thousands of people - officials, soldiers, tribute-bearers, priests, servants - would have filled the terraces and courtyards. Administrative tablets found at Persepolis record rations issued to workers and travelers passing through the site, giving us a glimpse of the vast organizational effort required to sustain the court's operations.

At the center of it all was the king himself, and his presence was governed by elaborate protocol designed to amplify his authority at every moment. Audiences with the king followed strict rules. Approaching the royal person required specific gestures of submission - prostration, in some cases, a practice the Greeks found deeply alien and called *proskynesis*. The king sat elevated, often beneath a canopy, visually separated from those who came before him. Even high officials and foreign ambassadors were made to feel the distance between themselves and the throne.

This was not mere vanity. It was political technology. By making access to the king rare, controlled, and ritually charged, the court transformed every royal audience into an event of enormous consequence. To be received by the king was a privilege. To be ignored by him was a sentence.

A Multicultural Court

One of the most striking features of Achaemenid court culture was its deliberate embrace of diversity - not as a concession to the empire's many peoples, but as a demonstration of royal power over them.

The reliefs at Persepolis make this explicit. Rather than depicting subject peoples as defeated enemies - as Egyptian or Assyrian royal art so often did - the Apadana carvings show them as orderly participants in a shared imperial order. They bring gifts. They walk in procession. They are part of the king's world, not crushed beneath his feet.

This was a sophisticated ideological choice. The Achaemenid kings styled themselves not as conquerors of foreign peoples but as legitimate rulers of each people's own traditions. Darius I presented himself as a proper pharaoh in Egypt, a protector of Babylonian temples in Mesopotamia, and a defender of Persian religious traditions at home. The court reflected this multiplicity: officials, craftsmen, and advisors came from across the empire, and the art they produced blended Persian, Elamite, Babylonian, Egyptian, and Greek influences into something distinctly Achaemenid.

The result was a court culture that was, paradoxically, both deeply hierarchical and genuinely cosmopolitan.

The Experience of Royal Grandeur

What did it feel like to stand in the Apadana and look up?

No first-person account from an ancient visitor survives in full, but the physical evidence speaks clearly enough. The columns were painted. The stone reliefs were colored - traces of pigment have been found, suggesting that what we now see as pale limestone was once vivid with reds, blues, and greens. The floors may have been covered with carpets. The king's throne gleamed with gold and precious stones.

Add to this the sound of a court in full ceremony - the movement of thousands of people, the presence of musicians, the smell of incense - and the Apadana becomes something almost impossible to reconstruct from its ruins alone. It was designed to overwhelm every sense simultaneously, to make the individual feel small and the king feel infinite.

Greek visitors, who left some of the most detailed outside accounts of the Persian court, were simultaneously dazzled and unsettled. They admired the wealth and the organization. They were troubled by the submission it demanded. Their discomfort tells us something important: Persepolis worked exactly as intended. It produced a reaction. It made people feel something they could not easily shake.

Legacy in Stone and Risk

Persepolis burned in 330 BCE, when Alexander the Great's forces sacked and torched the palace complex - an act that ancient sources variously describe as deliberate revenge for the Persian burning of Athens, or as a drunken accident, or as both. Whatever the cause, the fire ended Persepolis as a living royal center.

But it did not erase it.

The ruins survived, and they have fascinated visitors, scholars, and conquerors ever since. Today, Persepolis stands as a UNESCO World Heritage Site, recognized as one of the most significant archaeological complexes in the world. Its carved reliefs remain among the finest examples of ancient art anywhere - detailed, expressive, and remarkably well-preserved in places.

Yet the site faces real threats. Environmental factors, tourism pressure, and regional instability all pose risks to the physical fabric of what remains. Some of the distinctive column capitals - those double-headed animal sculptures that once crowned the Apadana's towering columns - are particularly vulnerable. Preserving Persepolis is not merely an archaeological concern. It is a question of whether one of humanity's most eloquent statements about power, art, and empire will survive for future generations to read.

Key Takeaways

- **Persepolis was a ceremonial complex**, not an administrative capital - it was designed to perform imperial power through architecture, art, and ritual.

- **Construction began under Darius I** and was continued and expanded by his successor Xerxes, spanning the height of Achaemenid power.

- **The Apadana**, the great audience hall, featured thirty-six towering columns and processional reliefs depicting tribute-bearers from twenty-three subject peoples.

- **Susa served as the empire's administrative heart**, handling governance, correspondence, and taxation while Persepolis handled ceremony.

- **Royal audiences were highly ritualized**, using protocol, physical elevation, and controlled access to amplify the king's authority.

- **Achaemenid court culture was deliberately multicultural**, presenting the empire's diversity as evidence of royal power rather than a challenge to it.

- **Persepolis was destroyed by Alexander the Great in 330 BCE** but survives as a UNESCO World Heritage Site and remains at risk from environmental and human pressures.

- **The site's carved reliefs** offer direct visual evidence of how the Achaemenid kings understood and projected their own power.

What Persepolis ultimately reveals is that the Achaemenid kings understood something many rulers before and after them missed: power is not only exercised, it is *experienced*. The empire's strength lay not just in its armies or its tax revenues, but in its ability to make people feel - viscerally, in their bodies, standing at the foot of those limestone stairs - that the world had a center, and that the king stood at it. That insight, carved into stone and painted in brilliant color, outlasted the empire itself by more than two millennia. How empires hold together across such vast distances, and what happens when those bonds begin to fray, would prove to be the central challenge not only of Persia but of every great power that followed.

Chapter 11
Religion and Royal Ideology

When Darius I stood before his subjects as king of the largest empire the world had yet seen, he did not claim power through conquest alone. He claimed it through the gods - or more precisely, through one god above all others. "By the grace of Ahura Mazda," his inscriptions repeat, again and again, carved into cliff faces and palace walls across the Persian heartland. That phrase was not decoration. It was the foundation of everything.

The Weight of Divine Sanction

To rule an empire stretching from the Aegean coast to the Indus River - from Egypt in the west to Central Asia in the east - required more than armies and administrators. It required a story. Every great empire needs one: a narrative that explains why these particular people, under this particular king, have the right to govern everyone else. For the Achaemenid Persians, that story was written in the language of Zoroastrianism.

Between roughly 550 and 330 BCE, the Achaemenid Empire flourished as the dominant power of the ancient world. Its kings - Cyrus, Cambyses, Darius, Xerxes, and their successors - presided over dozens of conquered peoples, hundreds of languages, and an almost incomprehensible diversity of local customs and beliefs. Holding that together required administrative genius, yes. But it also required ideology. Religion gave the Achaemenid kings something no army could provide: moral authority.

Zoroastrianism shaped the way Persian kings understood themselves, presented themselves to their subjects, and justified their power. This is a story about faith, certainly - but also about politics, identity, and the enduring human need to believe that whoever holds power does so for a reason.

Zoroastrianism: The Faith at the Heart of Persia

Few religions in history have punched so far above their weight. Zoroastrianism is one of the world's oldest surviving monotheistic traditions, and its influence on later religious thought - on Judaism, Christianity, and Islam - is far greater than most people realize. Yet it remains relatively obscure to general readers, overshadowed by the faiths it helped shape.

At its core, Zoroastrianism centers on the worship of Ahura Mazda, the "Wise Lord," a supreme deity representing truth, light, and cosmic order. The religion was founded - or systematized - by the prophet Zarathustra, whose teachings form the basis of the Avesta, Zoroastrianism's sacred texts. The faith frames existence as a cosmic struggle between Ahura Mazda and Angra Mainyu, the destructive spirit of chaos and falsehood. Every human being, in this worldview, participates in that struggle through their choices - through truth or through lies, through righteousness or through corruption.

That ethical framework had enormous political implications. Truth - *asha* in the Avestan language - was not merely a personal virtue. It was a cosmic principle, the ordering force of the universe itself. And the king, in Zoroastrian thought, was its earthly champion.

Darius and the Official Embrace of the Faith

Darius I seized the Achaemenid throne in 522 BCE after a period of violent succession struggles. His rise to power was contested - he faced rebellions across the empire almost immediately - and he needed to establish his legitimacy quickly and decisively. Zoroastrianism gave him the tools to do it.

Darius officially adopted Zoroastrianism as the state religion of the Achaemenid Empire, and the consequences of that decision rippled outward through every dimension of Persian governance and culture. His great inscriptions - most famously the Behistun Inscription, carved high into a cliff in western Iran - invoke Ahura Mazda repeatedly, framing Darius's victories over his enemies not as political triumphs but as divine judgments. The rebels were liars, he declared. They had followed the Lie. Ahura Mazda had granted victory to Darius because Darius followed the Truth.

This was not merely rhetorical flourish. It was a complete ideological system. By aligning kingship with cosmic truth and opposition with cosmic falsehood, Darius transformed political rebellion into something close to sacrilege. To resist the king was to side with the forces of chaos against the divine order of the universe. That is a powerful message to send to a restless empire.

Fire, Stone, and Sacred Space

The physical landscape of the Achaemenid Empire bore witness to this religious vision. Fire temples - structures built to house and protect the sacred flame that burned as a symbol of Ahura Mazda's presence - appeared across the Persian heartland and beyond. Fire held a central place in Zoroastrian worship: it was pure, it gave light in darkness, and it could not be polluted in the way that earth or water might be. To tend the sacred flame was an act of devotion. To let it die was a kind of catastrophe.

These temples were not merely places of worship. They were statements of imperial identity, visible markers of the faith that undergirded Persian power. When Darius built at Persepolis - the great ceremonial capital whose ruins still stagger visitors today - he was constructing not just a palace complex but a theological argument rendered in stone. Reliefs lining the staircases at Persepolis show delegations from across the empire bringing tribute to the Persian king, an image of universal submission to a divinely sanctioned order.

Persepolis was, in this sense, a sacred space as much as a political one. The king who received tribute there did so as the representative of Ahura Mazda on earth.

The Ethics of Empire

What made Zoroastrian royal ideology distinctive - and historically significant - was its ethical dimension. Many ancient empires justified conquest through raw power or the favor of capricious gods. The Achaemenid framework was more sophisticated. Ahura Mazda was a god of justice and truth, and his earthly representative was therefore obligated to govern justly.

This had practical consequences. Achaemenid kings, particularly Cyrus the Great and Darius I, developed a reputation in the ancient world for a degree of tolerance toward conquered peoples that was unusual for the era. Cyrus famously allowed the Jews exiled in Babylon to return to their homeland and rebuild their temple - an act so remarkable that the Hebrew Bible refers to him as a messiah, an anointed one.

Whether this tolerance was primarily religious conviction, political pragmatism, or some combination of both is a question historians continue to debate. But the Zoroastrian emphasis on truth, justice, and the proper ordering of society almost certainly provided an ideological framework within which such policies made sense.

An empire that claimed to rule in the name of cosmic order had an interest, at least rhetorically, in maintaining order. That meant allowing subject peoples to live according to their own customs, worship their own gods, and manage their own local affairs, so long as they paid their taxes and acknowledged Persian supremacy. The philosophy of *asha* - righteous truth - demanded a king who was more than a conqueror. It demanded a guardian.

Kingship as Cosmic Duty

The relationship between the Persian king and Ahura Mazda was not a simple transaction - the god grants victory, the king offers sacrifice. It was something closer to a covenant, a mutual obligation embedded in the structure of the universe itself. The king was chosen by Ahura Mazda, but that choice came with responsibilities. He was expected to uphold truth, suppress the Lie, protect the weak, and maintain the proper order of things.

This idea - that royal power is not merely a privilege but a sacred duty - runs through Persian royal inscriptions with remarkable consistency. Darius does not merely boast of his conquests; he explains them. He was fighting the Lie. He was restoring order. He was fulfilling the will of Ahura Mazda. Every military campaign becomes, in this framing, a moral crusade.

Later Persian literature developed these themes in extraordinary ways. The *Shahnameh*, the great Persian epic composed by the poet Ferdowsi around 1000 CE but drawing on far older traditions, is saturated with the idea that legitimate kingship is inseparable from divine favor and moral virtue. The kings of the *Shahnameh* possess a quality called *farr* - a kind of divine radiance or royal glory, granted by Ahura Mazda to righteous rulers and withdrawn from those who fall into corruption or injustice. When a king loses his *farr*, his reign is finished, regardless of his armies or his wealth. The cosmos itself has withdrawn its sanction.

This concept of *farr* almost certainly has deep roots in Zoroastrian theology, and it illustrates how thoroughly religious ideas had penetrated Persian conceptions of legitimate power. A king was not simply a man who had seized the throne. He was a man whom the divine order had chosen - and that choice could be revoked.

Unifying a Diverse Empire

One of the most pressing challenges facing any ancient empire was the problem of diversity. How do you hold together dozens of different peoples, languages, and traditions under a single political authority without constant rebellion? The Achaemenids found part of their answer in Zoroastrianism - not by imposing the faith on conquered peoples, but by using its ethical framework to articulate a vision of imperial order that could accommodate difference.

Zoroastrianism's emphasis on truth and justice provided a common moral vocabulary for the empire's ruling class, even as subject peoples continued to worship their own gods. The Persian king could present himself as a universal figure - a champion of cosmic order - rather than merely the leader of one ethnic group imposing its will on others. This was a more sophisticated form of imperial legitimacy than simple conquest, and it contributed meaningfully to the empire's remarkable cohesion and longevity.

The Achaemenid Empire lasted for more than two centuries, an extraordinary achievement given its size and diversity. No single factor explains that durability, but the ideological work done by Zoroastrianism - providing a moral framework for kingship, a shared identity for the Persian ruling class, and a vocabulary of justice that could be extended to subject peoples - was a significant part of the story.

Legacy: A Faith That Shaped the World

When Alexander the Great destroyed Persepolis in 330 BCE, he ended the Achaemenid Empire but could not erase what it had built. Zoroastrianism survived, continuing to shape Persian identity through the Parthian and Sasanian periods and beyond. Its theological concepts - the cosmic struggle between good and evil, the resurrection of the dead, the final judgment, the coming of a savior figure - entered the bloodstream of Western religious thought, influencing Jewish apocalyptic literature, early Christianity, and eventually Islam.

The idea that a ruler governs by divine sanction, that power carries moral obligation, that the cosmos itself has a stake in how human beings treat one another - these are not uniquely Zoroastrian ideas, but Zoroastrianism gave them some of their earliest and most sophisticated political expression. When Darius carved "by the grace of Ahura Mazda" into the rock at Behistun, he was doing something that rulers across the ancient and medieval world would do in their own ways, in their own languages, for millennia to come.

Quick Summary

- Zoroastrianism, centered on the worship of Ahura Mazda and the cosmic principle of truth (*asha*), became the official state religion of the Achaemenid Empire under Darius I.

- Darius used Zoroastrian ideology to legitimize his contested rule, framing his kingship as divinely sanctioned and his enemies as agents of cosmic falsehood.

- Fire temples and monumental architecture - including the ceremonial capital at Persepolis - gave physical form to the empire's religious identity.

- Zoroastrian ethics emphasized truth, justice, and righteous governance, providing an ideological framework that supported relatively tolerant policies toward conquered peoples.

- The concept of *farr* - divine royal glory - embedded in Persian tradition held that legitimate kingship depended on moral virtue, not merely military power.

- Zoroastrian religious ideas contributed to the Achaemenid Empire's cohesion by providing a shared moral vocabulary for its ruling class across a vast and diverse territory.

- Zoroastrianism's theological concepts - cosmic dualism, divine judgment, a coming savior - had a lasting influence on Judaism, Christianity, and Islam, making it one of the most consequential religious traditions in world history.

What Darius understood, and what the Achaemenid experiment demonstrated, is that empires are not built on force alone. They are built on stories - stories about why power exists, who deserves it, and what it is for. Zoroastrianism gave the Persian kings a story powerful enough to hold the ancient world together for two centuries. The echoes of that story, refracted through the faiths it influenced and the political traditions it helped shape, have never entirely faded.

Chapter 12
A Diverse Empire

Somewhere in the administrative heart of Persepolis, a scribe pressed a stylus into a clay tablet and recorded the daily rations for a group of workers - not Persian warriors or noble courtiers, but Egyptian craftsmen, Babylonian laborers, Lydian stonecutters, and Indian elephant handlers, all drawing wages from the same imperial treasury. They came from the edges of the known world. They spoke different languages, prayed to different gods, and ate different food. And yet they worked, side by side, under the same king.

That image - mundane, bureaucratic, almost accidental in its intimacy - captures something essential about the Achaemenid Empire that grand military narratives tend to miss. This was not simply an empire of conquest. It was an empire of coexistence, one that stretched from the Aegean coast to the Indus Valley and managed, for a time, to hold together one of the most ethnically and culturally varied populations the ancient world had ever seen. How it did so, and what daily life actually looked like for the millions of people living within its borders, is the story this chapter tells.

An Empire Built on Difference

When Cyrus the Great founded the Achaemenid Empire in the 550s BC, he inherited a world already dense with ancient civilizations. Lydia had its own kings, its own coinage, its own gods. Babylon had its temples and its centuries of written law. Egypt had its pharaohs and its priesthood. Rather than bulldozing these traditions and imposing a single Persian identity, Cyrus made a calculated and, as it turned out, remarkably effective choice: he let them be.

This was not sentimentality. It was strategy. An empire that allowed conquered peoples to maintain their languages, worship their gods, and observe their customs was an empire that spent less energy suppressing rebellion and more energy collecting taxes and building roads. Cyrus understood - or at least intuited - that legitimacy was cheaper than coercion.

His successors inherited this approach and, in many cases, deepened it. Darius I, who came to power in the late 6th century BC and oversaw some of the empire's most ambitious administrative reforms, institutionalized what Cyrus had practiced informally. Under Darius, the empire was divided into satrapies - regional administrative units, each governed by a satrap who was typically a Persian noble but who operated within a local cultural context. The satrap collected tribute, maintained order, and reported to the king. But the farmers still farmed their ancestral land, the priests still conducted their ancestral rites, and the merchants still traded in their ancestral languages.

The Satrapy System: Local Power, Imperial Logic

At its height, the Achaemenid Empire contained somewhere around twenty to thirty satrapies, each one a world unto itself. Lydia, in western Anatolia, was a prosperous region with a long tradition of commerce - the Lydians are often credited with inventing coinage, and that innovation, absorbed into the imperial economy, helped standardize trade across vast distances. Babylonia, in Mesopotamia, was one of the wealthiest and most urbanized regions in the ancient world, home to merchants, astronomers, and temple administrators whose records stretched back centuries. Egypt, when it fell under Persian control, retained its priestly class and its deeply rooted religious institutions.

What held these wildly different places together was not cultural uniformity but administrative coherence. Darius built the Royal Road - a roughly 1,600-mile artery connecting Susa in the Persian heartland to Sardis in western Anatolia - which allowed royal messengers to travel its length in about a week. Information moved. Tribute moved.

Soldiers moved. And with them moved ideas, goods, and people.

The empire also developed a sophisticated system of record-keeping. Clay tablets from Persepolis - known as the Persepolis Fortification Tablets - document in extraordinary detail the movement of workers, the distribution of rations, and the management of resources across the imperial core. These are not heroic documents. They are receipts, work orders, and payroll records. But they reveal an empire that was, at its administrative heart, genuinely cosmopolitan.

Daily Life: Workers, Artisans, and the People History Forgets

Most people who lived in the Achaemenid Empire were not kings or generals. They were farmers, potters, weavers, bakers, and builders. While the historical record is thinner for these lives than for the lives of the powerful, the Persepolis tablets offer a rare window into the working world of the ancient Near East.

Workers at Persepolis received rations of grain, wine, and sometimes beer, distributed according to their skill level and the nature of their work. Skilled craftsmen - stonemasons, metalworkers, carpenters - received more than unskilled laborers. Workers from different regions of the empire appear in the records: Egyptians, Babylonians, Lydians, Cappadocians, and others, all documented with a bureaucratic thoroughness that suggests the Persian administration took its workforce seriously.

Artisans occupied a particularly valued place in this world. The construction of Persepolis itself - that vast ceremonial complex of columned halls, sculpted staircases, and carved reliefs - drew craftsmen from across the empire. The reliefs that line the staircases of the Apadana, Persepolis's great audience hall, depict delegations from dozens of subject peoples, each rendered in their distinctive dress, each bearing gifts appropriate to their homeland. Scholars read these images as a kind of visual inventory of the empire's diversity -

a deliberate statement, carved in stone, that this king ruled not one people but many.

Women in the Achaemenid World

One of the more striking revelations of the Persepolis tablets is the presence of women in the imperial workforce - and not merely as background figures. Women appear in the records as workers, supervisors, and recipients of rations. Some female workers received the same rations as their male counterparts. Others held supervisory roles, overseeing groups of other workers.

Women of the royal household wielded a different kind of influence. Queens and royal mothers in the Achaemenid court were not simply decorative figures. They managed estates, controlled resources, and participated in the political life of the court in ways that ancient sources, though often fragmentary, make clear. The mother of a king, in particular, could hold enormous informal authority - a pattern visible across several generations of Achaemenid rule.

Beyond the palace, women's roles varied enormously depending on their social class, their ethnic background, and their region of the empire. In Babylonia, women had long held legal rights to own property and conduct business, and these traditions continued under Persian rule. In other parts of the empire, women's lives were shaped by local customs that the Persian administration largely left intact. The empire did not impose a single model of womanhood any more than it imposed a single religion or a single language.

A Mosaic of Languages and Faiths

Walk through any major city of the Achaemenid Empire - Susa, Babylon, Sardis, Memphis - and you would have heard a babel of languages. Aramaic served as the empire's administrative lingua franca, the language of bureaucracy and long-distance communication. But Elamite, Babylonian, Egyptian, Greek, Lydian, and dozens of other languages continued to be spoken, written, and used in local contexts.

This linguistic pluralism was matched by religious diversity. The Persians themselves followed Zoroastrianism, with its emphasis on the cosmic struggle between truth and falsehood, light and darkness. But Cyrus famously allowed the Babylonians to worship Marduk, their chief deity, and permitted the Jews exiled in Babylon to return to their homeland and rebuild their temple in Jerusalem. This act - recorded in the Hebrew Bible and confirmed by the Cyrus Cylinder, a clay barrel inscription discovered in the 19th century - became one of the most celebrated examples of ancient religious tolerance.

Darius continued this pattern. He made offerings to Egyptian gods when he visited Egypt, presenting himself as a legitimate pharaoh rather than a foreign conqueror. Across the empire, local temples received imperial support, and local priesthoods retained their authority. Persian kings understood that religion was not just a matter of personal belief - it was a source of social order, and disrupting it invited unrest.

The Limits of Tolerance

None of this should be mistaken for modern multiculturalism. Achaemenid tolerance had clear limits, and those limits were defined by power.

Tribute was non-negotiable. Every satrapy paid into the imperial treasury, and the amounts were substantial. Herodotus, the Greek historian, recorded the tribute demands placed on each satrapy, and the figures suggest an empire extracting enormous wealth from its subject peoples. The roads and monuments that made the empire impressive were built on the labor and resources of millions who had no say in the matter.

Rebellion was met with force. When subject peoples rose against Persian authority - as they did on several occasions - the response could be swift and brutal. Tolerance extended to those who accepted Persian rule. Those who challenged it discovered the other face of empire.

And yet, within those constraints, the diversity of the Achaemenid Empire was real and, by the standards of the ancient world, remarkable. Peoples who had been conquered by previous empires - the Assyrians, for instance, who had a reputation for mass deportation and deliberate cultural destruction - found Persian rule comparatively light. The Persians took your tribute and your loyalty. They left you your gods.

Key Figures of the Diverse Empire

Cyrus the Great set the template. His conquest of Lydia in the 540s BC and his subsequent takeover of Babylon demonstrated that military victory could be followed by cultural accommodation rather than suppression. His approach to governance - respect local customs, co-opt local elites, present yourself as a liberator rather than a conqueror - became the foundational logic of Achaemenid rule.

Darius I systematized what Cyrus had improvised. His administrative reforms, his construction of the Royal Road, and his ambitious building programs at Persepolis and Susa transformed the empire from a collection of conquered territories into something approaching a coherent state. Darius also standardized coinage and weights and measures, making commerce across the empire's vast distances more practical. His reign, spanning the late 6th and early 5th centuries BC, marked the peak of Achaemenid administrative sophistication.

Legacy and Long-Term Impact

The Achaemenid model of empire - diverse, administratively coherent, tolerant of local difference within a framework of imperial authority - influenced the empires that came after it. When Alexander the Great conquered Persia in the 330s BC, he did not simply destroy what he found. He adopted much of it.

He kept Persian administrative structures, wore Persian dress, and attempted to present himself as a legitimate successor to the Achaemenid kings. The Seleucid Empire that followed, and later the Parthian and Sasanian empires, all inherited elements of the Persian approach to governing diverse populations.

The Cyrus Cylinder, rediscovered in the 19th century, became a touchstone for later discussions of human rights and religious freedom - a perhaps anachronistic reading, but one that speaks to how genuinely unusual Cyrus's approach seemed, even across millennia.

More broadly, the Achaemenid Empire demonstrated something that later empires would repeatedly have to relearn: that diversity, managed with intelligence and a degree of genuine respect, could be a source of strength rather than weakness. An empire that drew craftsmen from Egypt, merchants from Lydia, administrators from Babylon, and soldiers from a dozen other peoples was an empire with enormous human resources. The challenge was holding it together. For roughly two centuries, the Achaemenids managed it.

Quick Summary

- The Achaemenid Empire, founded by Cyrus the Great in the 550s BC, was one of the most ethnically and culturally diverse states in the ancient world, stretching from the Aegean to the Indus Valley.

- Cyrus established a policy of cultural accommodation - allowing conquered peoples to keep their languages, religions, and customs - that became the hallmark of Persian imperial rule.

- Darius I formalized this approach through administrative reforms, dividing the empire into satrapies governed by Persian nobles who operated within local cultural contexts.

- The Royal Road, built under Darius, connected the empire's heartland to its western frontier and enabled the rapid movement of information, goods, and people.

- The Persepolis Fortification Tablets reveal a cosmopolitan workforce of craftsmen and laborers drawn from across the empire, including women who worked, supervised, and received wages.

- Aramaic served as the administrative lingua franca, but dozens of local languages continued to be spoken and written throughout the empire.

- Persian religious tolerance - exemplified by Cyrus's support for Babylonian and Jewish religious practices - was strategic as much as principled, but its effects were real and widely recognized.

- The Achaemenid model of diverse, administratively coherent empire influenced Alexander the Great and the empires that followed, leaving a long shadow across the ancient world.

What the Achaemenid Empire ultimately built was not just a political structure but a way of imagining what empire could be - not the erasure of difference, but its management, and occasionally its celebration. The carved delegations on the staircase at Persepolis, each people rendered in their own dress bearing their own gifts, were not just decoration. They were a statement of purpose. When Alexander arrived two centuries later and stood in those same halls, he understood what he was looking at. He kept the structure. He kept the idea. And in doing so, he acknowledged that the Persians had figured out something worth preserving.

PART 5
WAR, DIPLOMACY, AND THE WORLD

Chapter 13
The Persian Military Machine

A soldier who fell in battle was replaced before his body grew cold. That was the legend - and perhaps the reality - behind the most feared fighting force of the ancient world. The Persians called them the *anûšiya*, the Immortals, and the name alone was enough to unsettle an enemy's nerve.

But the Immortals were only one piece of a military system so carefully constructed that it allowed a single empire to govern and defend territory stretching from the Aegean coast to the borders of India. Understanding Persian power means understanding not just who fought, but how they were organized, supplied, and deployed across distances that would have broken lesser states entirely.

The machinery beneath the spectacle - the structure of the Achaemenid army, the role and reputation of its elite core, and the strategic logic that sustained it - reveals Persia not merely as a military force but as something rarer: a sustained imperial project. The goal here is not to catalogue every campaign or count every casualty, but to understand *how* Persia fought, and why that mattered.

An Empire That Had to Move

Before any discussion of soldiers or tactics, consider the sheer geographic problem the Achaemenid Empire faced. At its height, it was the largest empire the ancient world had yet seen, encompassing dozens of distinct peoples, languages, climates, and terrains. Governing such a territory required administration. Defending it required something more.

Persian military power was not built around a single standing army waiting at the capital. It was built around *mobility* - the capacity to raise, move, and supply forces across enormous distances, often faster than enemies expected. This logistical sophistication was, in many ways, the empire's most underappreciated military achievement.

Roads mattered enormously. The Royal Road, stretching roughly 2,700 kilometers from Susa to Sardis, allowed not just the famous royal couriers to move with speed, but also armies, supplies, and imperial communications. A military force that could move predictably and be resupplied reliably was a military force that could project power. The Achaemenids understood this better than most of their contemporaries.

The Army's Composition: Diversity as Strength

What struck outside observers most about the Persian army was its sheer variety. This was not a homogeneous national force. It was a mosaic: cavalry from the eastern satrapies, infantry from the Levant, archers from the Iranian plateau, naval contingents from Phoenicia and Egypt. When Xerxes marched toward Greece in 480 BCE, ancient sources described a force drawn from dozens of subject peoples, each fighting in their own manner, with their own weapons, under their own commanders.

This diversity was not a weakness. It was a deliberate feature of Achaemenid imperial strategy.

By incorporating subject peoples into the military structure, the empire accomplished several things at once. It reduced the burden on the Persian heartland to supply all manpower. It gave conquered peoples a stake in imperial success. And it created an army whose combined capabilities - heavy infantry, light cavalry, long-range archery, siege expertise - exceeded what any single military tradition could provide.

At the top of this layered structure sat the Persian and Median core: professional soldiers drawn from the empire's heartland, trained to a higher standard, and trusted with the most critical roles. Below them, in rough order of reliability and training, came the forces of allied and subject peoples. It was a pyramid, and the Immortals stood at its apex.

The Immortals: Myth and Reality

Ten thousand strong. Always ten thousand. That was the principle behind the unit the Greeks called the *Athanatoi* - the Immortals. According to the Greek historian Herodotus, whenever one of their number was killed or fell ill, a replacement stepped forward immediately, so that the unit's strength never visibly diminished. Whether this happened with the clockwork precision the legend implies is difficult to verify, but the *system* behind it was real: the Immortals were a maintained, professional force with a defined and enforced strength.

They were drawn from the Persian and Median heartland - men selected not just for physical capability but for their connection to the empire's core identity. In a military built on multicultural contingents, the Immortals represented something specific: Persian loyalty, Persian discipline, and Persian prestige.

Their equipment reflected their dual role. Armed with spears, swords, and bows, they could fight at range or close quarters, adapting to battlefield conditions in ways that specialized units could not. This flexibility made them valuable both as shock troops in open battle and as a personal guard for the king himself - a role that carried enormous symbolic weight in a system where the monarch's safety and authority were inseparable.

That symbolic dimension deserves emphasis. The Immortals were not simply a military unit. They were a statement. Their presence on campaign communicated the king's personal investment in a conflict. Their discipline and uniformity - their very *immortality* - projected an image of an empire that could not be worn down, could not be depleted, would always replenish itself. In an era when psychological warfare was waged as much through reputation as through force, this mattered enormously.

Strategy and the Logic of Persian Power

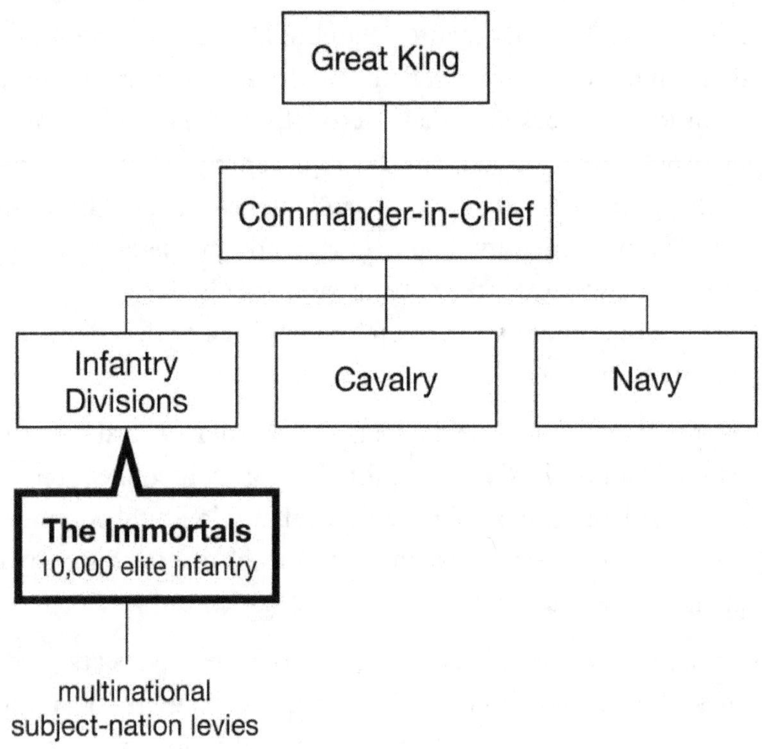

Structure of the Achaemenid army

Persian military strategy was shaped by the empire's fundamental character: vast, diverse, and dependent on maintaining order across enormous distances. This produced a strategic outlook that prioritized *deterrence* and *overwhelming force* over the kind of nimble, risk-taking aggression that characterized some of their opponents.

When the Achaemenids moved against an enemy, they typically moved with numbers and preparation meant to make resistance seem futile. The goal was not always to fight - it was often to make fighting unnecessary. Submission was preferable to conquest, because a submitted province still produced taxes, soldiers, and grain. A destroyed one produced nothing.

This logic shaped how Persian armies were assembled and deployed. Campaigns were preceded by extensive diplomatic activity - demands for earth and water, the symbolic tokens of submission. Military force followed only when diplomacy failed, and when it did, the force brought to bear was intended to be conclusive.

Logistics underpinned all of it. Feeding an army of tens of thousands across hundreds of kilometers required pre-positioned supply depots, organized requisitioning from local populations, and careful route planning. The same administrative infrastructure that ran the empire in peacetime - the satrapies, the royal roads, the courier system - became the backbone of military campaigns. War and governance, in the Achaemenid system, were not separate functions. They ran on the same machinery.

What Made Persian Power Durable

Armies win battles. Empires require something more sustained. What made the Achaemenid military machine genuinely impressive was not any single engagement but its *durability* - the capacity to absorb setbacks, reconstitute forces, and continue projecting power across generations.

The Immortals embodied this quality in miniature. A unit that maintained its strength regardless of losses was a unit that communicated permanence. And permanence - the sense that the empire would outlast any particular crisis - was itself a form of power. Subject peoples who might consider rebellion had to weigh their chances not just against the army currently in the field, but against an empire that would send another, and another after that.

This is why the Immortals' legacy extends beyond their battlefield record. They represented an institutional commitment to military excellence - a recognition that the empire's security depended on maintaining a professional core that could not be eroded by attrition. In a world where most armies were raised for specific campaigns and then disbanded, that kind of institutional continuity was genuinely unusual.

The multicultural composition of the broader army reinforced this durability in a different way. By drawing military manpower from across the empire, the Achaemenids ensured that no single region's losses could cripple the whole. The system was redundant by design. And redundancy, in military logistics as in engineering, is what separates structures that survive from those that collapse under pressure.

Legacy and Long-Term Impact

The Persian military system influenced successors who studied it carefully. When Alexander of Macedon dismantled the Achaemenid Empire in the 330s BCE, he did not simply discard what he found. He absorbed it. Persian administrative structures, Persian logistical methods, and even Persian soldiers found their way into the Macedonian war machine. The conqueror, in other words, recognized the value of what he had conquered.

The Immortals themselves passed into legend - a legend powerful enough that later empires reached back to claim the name. The Sassanid Persian Empire, centuries after the Achaemenids, maintained elite units that consciously echoed the tradition. The concept of a maintained, professional, symbolically significant royal guard proved durable across cultures and centuries.

What the Persian military machine ultimately demonstrated was a principle that transcends any particular era: sustained imperial power requires not just the ability to win battles, but the infrastructure to keep fighting them. Logistics, organization, and institutional memory - these are the unglamorous foundations on which military greatness is actually built.

Quick Summary

- **The Achaemenid army was deliberately multicultural**, drawing soldiers from across the empire's many subject peoples and combining diverse military traditions into a flexible fighting force.

- **The Royal Road and imperial infrastructure** were as important to Persian military power as any weapon - they allowed armies and supplies to move with speed across vast distances.

- **The Immortals were a maintained force of 10,000 elite soldiers**, drawn from the Persian and Median heartland, armed for both ranged and close combat, serving as both shock troops and royal guard.

- **Their "immortality" was institutional, not mythical -** replacements were integrated immediately to keep the unit at full strength, communicating permanence and resilience.

- **Persian strategy prioritized deterrence**, using overwhelming force and diplomatic pressure to make resistance seem futile before a battle was ever fought.

- **Logistics and administration formed the backbone of Persian campaigns**, with the same imperial infrastructure that governed the empire also supplying its armies.

- **The system's durability was its defining achievement** - the capacity to absorb losses, reconstitute forces, and project power across generations, not just campaigns.

- **Alexander's adoption of Persian methods** after his conquest confirmed what the Achaemenids had long demonstrated: organizational sophistication outlasts any single army in the field.

Persian military power was, at its core, a problem of scale solved through system. The Immortals captured the imagination of ancient observers - and have held it ever since - because they made that system visible and human. Ten thousand soldiers who could not be killed, drawn from the heart of an empire that seemed equally indestructible. The legend was exaggerated, as legends always are. But the reality it pointed toward was not. What the Achaemenids built was a military machine that ran on discipline, logistics, and institutional memory, and it ran with remarkable consistency for over two centuries. The armies that eventually brought it down had to become, in many ways, its students first.

Chapter 14
Persia and the Wider World

When Cyrus the Great rode into Babylon in 539 BCE, he did not arrive as a conqueror in the traditional sense. He arrived as a liberator, or at least, that is how he chose to present himself, and how many Babylonians chose to receive him. Within days, the most powerful city in the ancient world had changed hands without a battle worth recording. What followed was not plunder but policy: Cyrus restored temples, returned exiled peoples to their homelands, and issued proclamations in the local language. It was a masterclass in imperial statecraft, and it announced something the ancient world had not quite seen before - an empire that understood the power of inclusion.

For too long, the story of the Achaemenid Persian Empire has been filtered through a single lens: the Greek one. Herodotus, Thucydides, and the Athenian playwrights gave Western civilization its dominant image of Persia - an exotic, despotic East pressing against the heroic, freedom-loving West. Marathon. Thermopylae. Salamis. These battles became the founding myths of Western identity, and Persia became the villain of the story.

But that framing distorts far more than it reveals. From 550 BCE to 330 BCE, the Achaemenid Empire was the largest political entity the world had yet seen, stretching from the Aegean coast to the borders of India, from the steppes of Central Asia to the deserts of Egypt. It governed dozens of languages, hundreds of peoples, and millennia of accumulated civilizations. Greece was one frontier among many, and not even the most important one. To understand Persia on its own terms, we have to step back from the Athenian perspective and look at the full sweep of a world that Persia, more than any other power of its age, held together.

The World Persia Inherited

Before Cyrus, the ancient Near East was a patchwork of competing powers, each with its own imperial ambitions and long memories of domination. Assyria had terrorized the region for centuries, deporting populations and razing cities with systematic brutality. Babylon had risen to fill the vacuum after Assyria's collapse in the late seventh century. Egypt, ancient beyond reckoning, maintained its own rhythms along the Nile. Lydia, in western Anatolia, had grown wealthy on trade and was among the first states to mint coinage. And across the Iranian plateau, a collection of tribes and kingdoms - including the Medes, who had helped bring Assyria down - jostled for position.

The consolidation of the Iranian tribes under Persian leadership was not simply a story of ambition. It was, in part, a response to the instability that Assyrian aggression had created across the region. Communities that had been displaced, disrupted, and reorganized under Assyrian pressure needed new frameworks for survival and prosperity. Cyrus provided one.

When he founded the Achaemenid Empire around 550 BCE, Cyrus was not building from nothing. He was inheriting a world already dense with administrative traditions, trade networks, religious institutions, and diplomatic customs. His genius - and it was genuine - lay in recognizing that the fastest way to govern this world was not to replace these systems but to work through them.

Babylon: The Prize and the Partnership

No conquest shaped the early Achaemenid Empire more profoundly than the fall of Babylon. Babylon was not merely a city; it was a civilization in concentrated form. Its temples housed centuries of astronomical records. Its scribes maintained the most sophisticated bureaucratic traditions in the ancient world. Its merchants operated trade networks that stretched from the Persian Gulf to the Mediterranean.

Cyrus understood what he was acquiring. Rather than dismantling Babylonian institutions, he presented himself as the legitimate successor to the Babylonian kings - a servant of Marduk, the city's chief deity, rather than an alien conqueror. The famous Cyrus Cylinder, a clay document discovered in the nineteenth century, records his claims in Babylonian cuneiform: that Marduk had chosen him, that he had restored order, that he had returned displaced peoples to their homes.

Historians debate how much of this was genuine religious conviction and how much was calculated propaganda. Probably both. What matters is the result: Babylon became not a conquered province to be bled dry, but a functioning partner in the imperial project. Its administrative expertise, its scribal traditions, and its commercial networks were absorbed into the Achaemenid system, enriching the whole.

Egypt: Ancient Power, New Master

Egypt presented a different kind of challenge. When Cambyses II - Cyrus's son and successor - conquered Egypt in 525 BCE, he was absorbing a civilization that had been old when Babylon was young. Egypt's priests, bureaucrats, and regional elites had survived every previous foreign intrusion by outlasting it. They would try the same with Persia.

The Achaemenid approach to Egypt followed the Babylonian template. Persian kings presented themselves as pharaohs, adopted Egyptian royal titles, and made offerings to Egyptian gods. Darius I, who came to power in 522 BCE and would prove to be the empire's greatest organizer, was particularly attentive to Egyptian sensibilities. He completed a canal connecting the Nile to the Red Sea - a project that had been attempted before but never finished - and dedicated it with inscriptions in both Egyptian hieroglyphics and Persian cuneiform. It was an infrastructure project and a diplomatic statement at the same time.

Egypt was never fully comfortable under Persian rule, and revolts punctuated the relationship across the Achaemenid period. But the empire's willingness to accommodate local religious and cultural practices kept the relationship functional far longer than brute force alone could have managed.

Lydia: Gold, Coinage, and the Western Frontier

West of Babylon and north of Egypt lay Lydia, a kingdom in western Anatolia whose name had become synonymous with wealth. The Lydians, under their famously prosperous king Croesus, had developed one of the ancient world's first true coinage systems - standardized metal coins that made long-distance trade vastly more efficient. When Cyrus defeated Croesus around 547 BCE, he acquired not just territory but an economic infrastructure that would reshape Achaemenid commerce.

Lydia also brought Persia into direct contact with the Greek city-states along the Aegean coast. Many of these cities - Miletus, Ephesus, Sardis - had already been under Lydian influence and now passed into the Persian sphere. For most of the sixth century, this transition was relatively smooth. Greek merchants traded freely across the empire. Greek mercenaries served in Persian armies. Greek intellectuals, including some who would later shape Western philosophy, lived and worked in cities that were, technically, Persian imperial territory.

This is the context that the Greek-versus-Persian narrative so often obscures. For much of the Achaemenid period, the relationship between Persia and the Greek world was not one of civilizational conflict but of commercial entanglement, cultural exchange, and pragmatic coexistence.

The Greeks: One Frontier Among Many

The Persian Wars - the conflicts that produced Thermopylae and Salamis - occupy an outsized place in Western historical memory. From the Persian perspective, they were something rather different: a series of punitive campaigns against troublesome frontier peoples who had supported a rebellion in the empire's western provinces.

That rebellion - the Ionian Revolt of 499-493 BCE, in which Greek cities on the Anatolian coast rose against Persian rule - was the proximate cause of Darius I's famous expedition against mainland Greece. Athens had sent ships to support the rebels. Darius wanted accountability. His invasion of 490 BCE, which ended at Marathon, was not an attempt to conquer all of Europe. It was a targeted response to a specific provocation on a specific frontier.

Xerxes' larger invasion a decade later, in 480 BCE, was more ambitious - but even then, Greece represented one theater of imperial attention among many. Darius and Xerxes were simultaneously managing affairs in Egypt, suppressing revolts in Babylon, organizing the eastern frontiers near India, and maintaining the vast administrative machinery that kept the empire functioning. The Greek campaigns were significant, but they were not the empire's defining preoccupation.

When Persian forces withdrew after Salamis and Plataea, the empire did not collapse. It continued for another century and a half, largely intact, governing its hundreds of peoples with the same combination of accommodation and firm central authority that had characterized it from the start. The Greeks celebrated their victories as world-historical turning points. For Persia, they were setbacks on a distant frontier.

Diplomacy, Trade, and the Architecture of Empire

What made the Achaemenid Empire more than a collection of conquered territories was the infrastructure - physical, administrative, and diplomatic - that Darius I built to hold it together.

His Royal Road, stretching roughly 2,700 kilometers from Sardis in western Anatolia to Susa in southwestern Iran, was one of the ancient world's great engineering achievements. Relay stations positioned along its length allowed royal messengers to cover the entire distance in about a week - a speed of communication that gave the central government an unprecedented ability to project authority across vast distances. Merchants, diplomats, and armies all moved along the same arteries.

Darius also standardized weights and measures across the empire, facilitating trade between regions that had previously operated on incompatible systems. He developed the satrapy system - dividing the empire into provinces, each governed by a satrap who was responsible for tax collection, local administration, and military levies - while maintaining Persian oversight through royal inspectors known as "the eyes and ears of the king."

The result was an empire that could absorb enormous cultural diversity without fracturing. Aramaic served as the administrative lingua franca, allowing bureaucrats from Egypt to Bactria to communicate in a common written language even as they continued to speak their own tongues at home. Local religions were tolerated, local customs respected, and local elites incorporated into the imperial hierarchy wherever possible.

Cultural Exchange Across the Imperial World

Trade and administration were not the only things moving along those roads. Ideas traveled too.

Persian artistic styles absorbed and synthesized influences from every corner of the empire. The great ceremonial capital at Persepolis, begun under Darius I, employed craftsmen and materials from across the imperial world - Lebanese cedar, Egyptian stone-carvers, Lydian goldsmiths, Babylonian brick-makers. The result was an aesthetic that was distinctly Persian yet unmistakably cosmopolitan, a visual argument for the empire's breadth and ambition.

Religious ideas circulated as well. Zoroastrianism, the Persian faith centered on the cosmic struggle between truth and falsehood, influenced later religious traditions in ways that scholars are still tracing. The Achaemenid policy of religious tolerance - which allowed Babylonian priests to maintain their temples, Jewish exiles to return to Jerusalem, and Egyptian cults to continue uninterrupted - created conditions in which different theological traditions could encounter and influence one another.

This was not a multicultural utopia. The empire was built on conquest and maintained by the threat of force. Revolts were suppressed, sometimes harshly. But within the framework of imperial control, a degree of cultural exchange occurred that would have been impossible in a more fragmented world.

Legacy and Long-Term Impact

When Alexander of Macedon finally brought the Achaemenid Empire down between 334 and 330 BCE, he did not replace it with something entirely new. He stepped into its administrative structures, adopted many of its governing practices, and - in a move that would have seemed familiar to Cyrus - presented himself as a legitimate successor rather than a foreign destroyer.

That is perhaps the most telling measure of what the Achaemenids had built. Their empire was not just a military achievement; it was a template. The idea that a single political authority could govern diverse peoples through accommodation rather than erasure, that roads and common languages and standardized commerce could bind a continent together - these were Achaemenid innovations, and they outlasted the dynasty that created them.

Quick Summary

- The Achaemenid Persian Empire, founded by Cyrus the Great around 550 BCE, was the largest political entity the ancient world had yet produced, stretching from the Aegean to India.

- Cyrus's approach to conquest emphasized accommodation - preserving local institutions, religions, and elites rather than dismantling them, as demonstrated most clearly in Babylon.

- Egypt and Lydia were absorbed through similar strategies, with Persian kings adopting local royal titles and supporting local religious institutions to legitimize their rule.

- The Greek city-states represented one frontier among many; the Persian Wars were, from the Achaemenid perspective, punitive campaigns against rebellious western provinces rather than existential civilizational conflicts.

- Darius I transformed the empire's administration through the Royal Road, the satrapy system, standardized weights and measures, and Aramaic as a common administrative language.

- Cultural exchange across the empire was extensive - Persepolis itself was built by craftsmen from dozens of different peoples, and ideas, artistic styles, and religious concepts moved freely along imperial trade routes.

- When Alexander conquered the empire in 330 BCE, he largely preserved its administrative structures, a testament to how effectively the Achaemenid system had worked.

The Achaemenid Empire's greatest achievement was not any single battle or building, but the demonstration that diversity and coherence could coexist at continental scale. That lesson did not die with the dynasty. It echoed forward through every empire that came after - Roman, Byzantine, Islamic, Mongol - each one grappling, in its own way, with the same fundamental problem that Cyrus had first solved on the plains of Babylon: how to hold a world together without making it all the same.

PART 6
DECLINE AND FALL

Chapter 15
From Xerxes to Weakening Rule

When Xerxes returned from Greece in 479 BCE, he came back not as a conqueror but as a man who had watched his fleet burn at Salamis. The greatest empire the world had yet seen had reached its high-water mark, and the tide was already beginning to turn.

That retreat from Greece did not destroy the Achaemenid Empire. Nothing so dramatic happened so quickly. What followed instead was something slower, quieter, and in many ways more instructive: a long, structural unraveling that took place not on foreign battlefields but in palace corridors, provincial capitals, and the fractured loyalties of men who had once served a unified throne. Empires rarely collapse from a single blow. They hollow out first.

This chapter traces that hollowing, from the turbulent reign of Xerxes through the succession crises and regional revolts of the fourth century BCE, to the moment when Alexander of Macedon found not a fortress to storm but a structure already weakened from within.

The Weight of an Overextended World

To understand how the Achaemenid Empire began to fracture, it helps to remember how extraordinary its construction had been in the first place.

Cyrus the Great had built something without precedent. Between 550 and 530 BCE, he swept through Media, Lydia, and Babylon in a series of campaigns that redrew the map of the ancient world. His genius lay not only in military conquest but in the art of incorporation - allowing conquered peoples to retain their customs, their gods, and their local administrators, so long as tribute flowed and loyalty held.

Darius I, who came to power in 522 BCE after suppressing a wave of internal revolts, transformed that loose network of conquests into something resembling a functioning state. He formalized the satrapy system, dividing the empire into provinces each governed by a satrap - a royal appointee who collected taxes, maintained order, and answered to the king. He built the Royal Road, stretching roughly 2,700 kilometers from Sardis to Susa, allowing messages and armies to move with remarkable speed. He introduced the gold daric, a standardized coinage that helped bind together an economy spanning three continents.

By the time Darius handed power to his son Xerxes in 486 BCE, the Achaemenid Empire was the largest political entity the world had ever known. It was also, by that very fact, extraordinarily difficult to hold together.

Xerxes and the Limits of Ambition

Xerxes I inherited an empire already showing signs of strain. Egypt had revolted. Babylon had revolted. His father had died before he could personally lead the punitive campaign against Athens - the city that had humiliated Persia at Marathon in 490 BCE. Xerxes moved to crush these rebellions first, then turned his attention westward.

His invasion of Greece in 480 BCE was the largest military expedition the ancient world had witnessed. Persian forces crossed the Hellespont on a bridge of boats, marched through Thrace and Macedonia, and pushed south through the famous pass at Thermopylae, where a small Spartan-led force held them for three days before being outflanked. Athens was sacked. It must have seemed, briefly, like total victory.

Then came Salamis.

In the narrow straits off the Athenian coast, the Greek fleet - smaller, more maneuverable, fighting in waters it knew - shattered the Persian navy. Xerxes watched from a throne on the shore. The following year, at Plataea, Persian land forces were defeated decisively. The western campaign was over.

Xerxes returned to Persia and, by most accounts, largely withdrew from active military command. He turned instead to building projects - most famously at Persepolis, where construction continued on the grand ceremonial complex his father had begun. But the palace, however magnificent, could not substitute for the political authority that was quietly eroding around him.

In 465 BCE, Xerxes was assassinated - killed in a palace conspiracy that involved members of his own court. His son Artaxerxes I came to power not through orderly succession but through the violent removal of rivals. It was a pattern that would repeat.

The Machinery of Decline

What makes the post-Xerxes period so historically revealing is that the empire did not fall apart all at once. It continued to function. Taxes were collected. Satraps governed. Trade moved along the Royal Road. From a distance, the Achaemenid state still looked like an empire.

But several structural problems were compounding simultaneously.

The satrapy system, designed for stability, became a source of fragmentation. Satraps governed enormous territories with considerable autonomy. Under strong kings, that autonomy was a feature - it allowed local administration without constant royal intervention. Under weaker kings, it became a liability. Satraps accumulated personal wealth, raised their own armies, and in some cases acted more like independent rulers than royal appointees. The further a province sat from Persepolis or Susa, the more loosely the king's authority was felt.

Succession crises became chronic. The Persian court did not operate under a clear principle of primogeniture. Multiple sons of the king could claim legitimacy, and the result was that each royal death risked triggering a violent contest for power. Court factions - eunuchs, generals, royal wives, ambitious nobles - maneuvered constantly. The assassination of Xerxes was not an aberration. It was a preview.

Heavy taxation fed resentment. The empire's administrative sophistication required revenue, and that revenue came from subject peoples across an enormous geographic range. Economic difficulties, combined with the perception that tribute flowed toward Persian elites rather than back into local communities, generated recurring grievances. Egypt in particular proved persistently restless, revolting multiple times across the fifth and fourth centuries BCE.

The Long Reign of Artaxerxes II and the Fracturing Fourth Century

If any single reign captures the texture of Achaemenid decline, it is that of Artaxerxes II, who ruled from 404 to 358 BCE - one of the longest reigns in the dynasty's history, and one of its most troubled.

He came to power immediately facing a challenge from his own brother, Cyrus the Younger, who raised a mercenary army - including the Greek soldiers famously described by the historian Xenophon - and marched against him. Cyrus was killed at the Battle of Cunaxa in 401 BCE, but the episode revealed something damaging: a Persian prince had been able to recruit a substantial Greek mercenary force and march deep into the empire's heartland before being stopped. The king's authority was not uncontested, even within his own family.

More of the same followed in the decades after Cunaxa. Regional revolts flared across the western satrapies. Egypt broke free and maintained its independence for much of this period. The empire's western frontier became a zone of persistent instability, with Greek city-states, Spartan ambitions, and restless satraps all complicating Persian control.

Artaxerxes III, who succeeded after another violent succession, briefly reversed some of this fragmentation - reconquering Egypt in 343 BCE and reasserting central authority with considerable brutality. But he too was assassinated, in 338 BCE, and the dynasty entered its final, chaotic phase.

How an Empire Hollows Out

By the time Alexander of Macedon crossed the Hellespont in 334 BCE, the Achaemenid Empire had been weakening for generations. That is not to diminish Alexander's military genius - his campaigns were genuinely extraordinary. But he was not breaking a healthy structure. He was accelerating the collapse of one already compromised.

Darius III, the last Achaemenid king, was not a weak man by temperament, but he ruled a system that had been undermined by a century of court intrigue, provincial fragmentation, and eroded central authority. He lost the Battle of Issus in 333 BCE, the Battle of Gaugamela in 331 BCE, and fled east, only to be murdered by his own satrap Bessus in 330 BCE. With his death, the dynasty ended - not with a final stand, but with a betrayal from within.

That betrayal was almost poetically appropriate. An empire that had spent decades consuming itself through internal conspiracy finally ended the same way.

Legacy and Long-Term Impact

The Achaemenid Empire's decline offers a case study that subsequent rulers studied, consciously or not, for centuries. Its administrative innovations - the satrapy system, standardized coinage, the Royal Road - were not discarded when Alexander conquered Persia. They were absorbed. Alexander and his successors adapted Persian administrative structures for their own purposes, and the Seleucid Empire that emerged from the wreckage owed more to Darius I's organizational genius than its Macedonian rulers typically acknowledged.

The empire's cultural legacy proved equally durable. Its model of tolerant, multi-ethnic governance - allowing subject peoples to maintain their languages, religions, and customs - influenced how later empires thought about the problem of ruling diverse populations. The Achaemenid approach was not altruistic; it was pragmatic. But pragmatism, in imperial administration, often outlasts ideology.

What the decline of the Achaemenid Empire ultimately demonstrates is that size alone does not sustain power. The same administrative complexity that made the empire function also made it vulnerable - to the ambitions of satraps, to the grievances of overtaxed provinces, to the dynastic violence that erupted whenever a king died without an uncontested heir. Strength and fragility can be built from the same materials.

Quick Summary

- Xerxes I's failed invasion of Greece (480-479 BCE) marked the end of Achaemenid westward expansion and the beginning of a long internal decline.

- His assassination in 465 BCE established a pattern of court conspiracy and violent succession that would recur throughout the fourth century BCE.

- The satrapy system, effective under strong kings, became a source of fragmentation as provincial governors accumulated independent power.

- Chronic succession crises, heavy taxation, and recurring regional revolts - particularly in Egypt - steadily eroded central authority.

- Artaxerxes II's reign (404-358 BCE) illustrated the empire's structural vulnerabilities, including the near-civil war launched by his brother Cyrus the Younger.

- By the time Alexander invaded in 334 BCE, the empire had been weakening for generations; internal collapse and external conquest reinforced each other.

- Darius III, the last Achaemenid king, was murdered by his own satrap in 330 BCE - an ending that reflected the dynasty's long internal fracturing as much as Alexander's military brilliance.

- Achaemenid administrative innovations, including the satrapy system and standardized coinage, survived the empire's fall and shaped successor states for centuries.

Alexander's conquest is often told as the story of a young genius overwhelming an ancient power. But the more you look at the century before his arrival, the more the story shifts. The Achaemenid Empire did not simply fall to Macedonia - it had been falling, slowly and structurally, for decades. What Alexander found at the end of his march was not a wall but a door already swinging open. The question of what comes next - how the world reorganized itself after Persia - is where the story takes its next turn.

Chapter 16
The Last Empire of the Persians

When Alexander of Macedon rode into Persepolis in the winter of 330 BCE, he did not find a broken people. He found a civilization two centuries in the making - one that had absorbed Lydians and Babylonians, Egyptians and Indians, and made them all, in some meaningful sense, Persian. What he destroyed that night, when flames consumed the great palace of Xerxes, was not merely a building. It was a world.

That world tends to be told from the winner's perspective. Greek sources dominate the surviving record, and they cast Alexander as a liberator, a visionary, a god-touched conqueror spreading enlightenment across the East. But the Achaemenid Empire had its own logic, its own grandeur, and its own understanding of what it meant to rule. To grasp what was truly lost in 330 BCE - and what, against all odds, survived - we need to look at the conquest not through Macedonian eyes, but through Persian ones.

What follows is the story of how the greatest empire the ancient world had yet seen came to its end, what that ending looked like from the inside, and why the Persian legacy proved far more durable than any conqueror's ambition.

An Empire Built to Last

For two hundred years, the Achaemenid Empire stood as the largest political structure the world had ever known. Founded by Cyrus the Great around 550 BCE, it stretched at its height from the Aegean coast of Anatolia to the Indus Valley - a landmass encompassing dozens of languages, religions, and peoples. No single army had ever governed so much territory for so long.

What made the Achaemenid system work was not brute force alone. Cyrus had established a governing philosophy that was, by ancient standards, remarkably pragmatic. Conquered peoples were generally permitted to keep their gods, their customs, and their local administrators. The Persians installed satraps - regional governors - to collect taxes and maintain order, but they rarely demanded cultural submission. A Babylonian could worship Marduk. An Egyptian could honor Amun. The empire asked for loyalty and tribute, not conversion.

This tolerance was not sentimentality. It was statecraft. An empire that did not constantly inflame local resentment was an empire that did not constantly have to suppress rebellion. For most of its existence, the Achaemenid system worked exactly as designed.

By the time Darius III inherited the throne in 336 BCE, however, the empire was showing the strain of its own scale. Court intrigue had destabilized the succession. Western satrapies had grown accustomed to a degree of autonomy that made rapid military coordination difficult. And from the northwest, a new kind of threat was forming - one that moved faster, hit harder, and fought with a tactical ferocity the Persian military had not encountered before.

The Storm from Macedonia

Alexander became king of Macedon in 336 BCE, the same year Darius III came to power in Persia. He was twenty years old. Within two years, he had crossed the Hellespont with roughly 40,000 soldiers and begun what he framed as a war of Greek vengeance against the Persian Empire - retribution, he claimed, for Xerxes' invasion of Greece a century and a half earlier.

The framing was political theater, and most people on both sides probably knew it. Alexander wanted conquest, not justice. But the rhetoric gave his campaign a moral shape that Greek audiences could embrace.

What followed was a series of engagements that, in retrospect, seem almost impossibly swift. At the Granicus River in 334 BCE, Alexander defeated a Persian force in western Anatolia. At Issus in 333 BCE, he met Darius III himself on the battlefield and routed the Persian army, capturing the king's family in the process. At Gaugamela in 331 BCE - fought on a plain near modern-day northern Iraq - the two men faced each other again, and again Alexander prevailed. Darius fled east. His empire, for all practical purposes, had ceased to function as a unified state.

From a Persian perspective, these defeats were not simply military failures. They represented the collapse of an entire system of meaning. The Persian king was not merely a political leader - he was the earthly representative of Ahura Mazda, the supreme deity of Zoroastrian belief, the guardian of cosmic order. When Darius fled the field at Gaugamela, he was not just losing a battle. In the eyes of his subjects, he was abandoning the divine mandate that justified his rule.

The Fall of Persepolis

After Gaugamela, Alexander moved south toward the Persian heartland. He took Babylon without significant resistance. He entered Susa, one of the great royal capitals, and helped himself to its treasury. Then he turned toward Persepolis - the ceremonial heart of the Achaemenid world, the city where the kings of kings had received tribute from every corner of their empire.

Persepolis fell in early 330 BCE. What happened next remains one of the most debated acts of the ancient world. Alexander ordered the burning of the great palace complex - the same halls where Darius and Xerxes had held court, where the famous reliefs showed delegations from across the empire bearing gifts to the Persian throne. Ancient sources offer different explanations: some say it was a deliberate act of symbolic vengeance for the Persian burning of

Athens in 480 BCE; others suggest it was an impulsive act during a night of heavy drinking.

Whatever the cause, the effect was permanent. The palace burned. And with it burned the most visible symbol of Achaemenid power.

Darius III did not survive to see what came next. Fleeing eastward through the Iranian plateau, he was murdered by his own satraps - men who had calculated that a dead king was more useful to them than a living one, since they might negotiate with Alexander over a corpse but not over a rival claimant. When Alexander found Darius's body, he reportedly covered it with his own cloak and ordered a royal burial. It was a gesture of respect, but also of finality. The last Achaemenid king was gone.

What the Persians Lost - and What They Knew

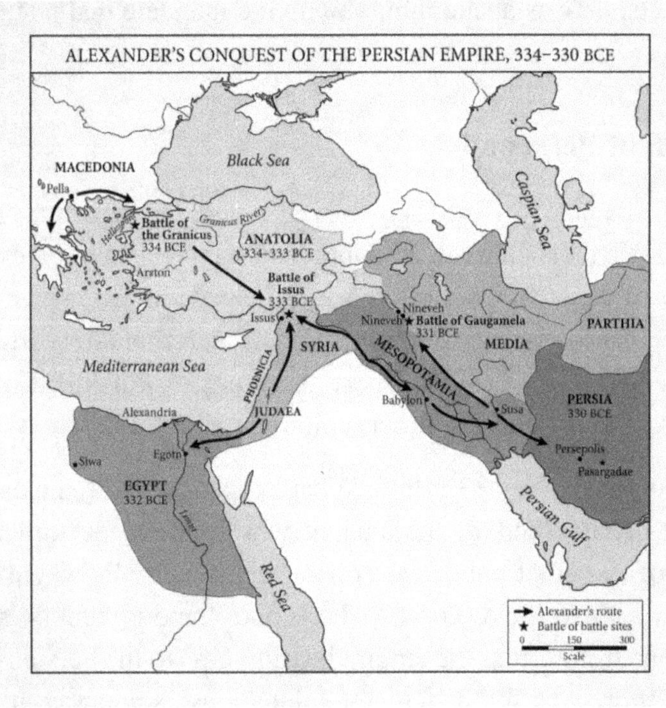

Alexander's conquest of the Persian Empire, 334–330 BCE

For the Persian nobility, the conquest was a catastrophe measured not only in political terms but in existential ones. The Achaemenid royal family had ruled for over two centuries. Their claim to power rested on divine favor, ancestral legitimacy, and the visible grandeur of their court. All of that evaporated within a few years of Alexander's crossing into Asia.

Yet the Persian response to conquest was more complex than simple submission. Many members of the Persian elite adapted with striking speed. Persian nobles served in Alexander's army. Persian administrators continued to manage the same provinces they had governed under the Achaemenids. Persian customs, dress, and court ceremonial began to influence Alexander himself - a development that scandalized many of his Macedonian officers, who felt their king was "going native."

Alexander's adoption of Persian royal dress and protocol was not vanity. He understood, as any competent ruler must, that governing a Persian empire required speaking Persian political language. He retained the satrapal system. He married Roxana, a Bactrian noblewoman, and later took Persian wives as well. He encouraged his officers to do the same. The conquest, in practice, became something more complicated than replacement - it became a negotiation between two civilizations, conducted at the level of dress, ritual, marriage, and administration.

From the Persian side, this negotiation carried its own ambiguities. Accepting Alexander's rule meant survival, and for many it meant continued influence. But it also meant watching a foreigner sit on the throne that had once belonged to Cyrus, Darius, and Xerxes - men whose names still carried the weight of legend.

What Survived the Fire

Empires fall. Civilizations are harder to kill.

The Persian cultural inheritance proved remarkably resilient in the face of Macedonian conquest. The Zoroastrian religious tradition, which had provided the Achaemenid kings with their theological framework, continued to flourish across the Iranian plateau. Persian artistic and architectural traditions did not vanish - they merged, transformed, and re-emerged in the hybrid forms that would characterize the Hellenistic world Alexander's conquests created.

The very cosmopolitanism that had defined the Achaemenid Empire at its height - its willingness to absorb and adapt rather than erase - now served the Persian people in their moment of subjugation. A civilization practiced in cultural flexibility was better equipped to survive conquest than one that had staked everything on rigid distinctiveness.

Greek influence did spread widely in the wake of Alexander's campaigns, as it was bound to do when Greek-speaking soldiers, merchants, and administrators flooded into formerly Persian territories. Cities were founded on the Greek model. Greek became a language of commerce and administration across a vast region. But this was never a simple replacement of Persian by Greek. What emerged was a blended world - Hellenistic in its surface forms, deeply Persian in many of its underlying structures.

The Seleucid Empire, which inherited much of Alexander's eastern territory after his death in 323 BCE, governed through institutions that owed as much to Achaemenid precedent as to Macedonian practice. And when the Parthians eventually displaced the Seleucids in the Iranian heartland during the third and second centuries BCE, they consciously positioned themselves as heirs to the Persian tradition - proof that the Achaemenid legacy had not been extinguished, only temporarily interrupted.

The Persian Perspective, Reconsidered

Greek and Roman writers shaped how the ancient world remembered Alexander's conquest, and they shaped it as triumph. But the Persian sources that survive - administrative records, religious texts, the testimony embedded in later Iranian literary tradition - suggest a more layered reality.

The Achaemenid Empire had not been a tyranny waiting to be overthrown. For most of its subjects, it had been a functioning order - imperfect, demanding, but also stable and, by ancient standards, relatively tolerant. Its fall did not feel like liberation to the Persians who lived through it. It felt like the end of a world.

And yet the world did not end. Persian identity, Persian religion, Persian artistic sensibility, and Persian administrative wisdom all outlasted the Achaemenid dynasty. They shaped the Hellenistic kingdoms that followed. They shaped the Parthian Empire. They would eventually shape the Sasanian Empire, which would present itself explicitly as the restoration of Persian greatness - and which would endure for another four centuries after that.

Alexander conquered Persia. But he could not unconquer what Persia had already made of the world.

Key Takeaways

- The Achaemenid Empire lasted from approximately 550 to 330 BCE, spanning over two centuries and encompassing an enormous range of peoples, languages, and cultures.

- Alexander's conquest was rapid and decisive: major Persian defeats at Granicus (334 BCE), Issus (333 BCE), and Gaugamela (331 BCE) effectively ended Achaemenid military resistance.

- The burning of Persepolis in 330 BCE destroyed the ceremonial heart of the empire and remains one of antiquity's most debated acts of destruction.

- Darius III, the last Achaemenid king, was murdered by his own satraps while fleeing Alexander - ending the royal line without a final stand.

- Alexander adopted significant elements of Persian court culture and administration, recognizing that governing a Persian empire required Persian political language.

- Persian cultural, religious, and administrative traditions survived the conquest and shaped the Hellenistic and Parthian worlds that followed.

- The fall of the Achaemenid Empire was not the end of Persian civilization - it was a rupture from which Persian identity eventually recovered and reasserted itself.

What Alexander destroyed at Persepolis could be measured in stone and timber. What he could not destroy was the accumulated memory of two centuries of Persian governance - the idea that a vast, diverse world could be held together not by enforced uniformity, but by a shared framework of order, tribute, and tolerance. That idea would outlast him by centuries, resurfacing in every empire that came after and tried, as the Persians had, to govern diversity at scale. The fire at Persepolis lit up the night sky over the Iranian plateau. But the

civilization it was meant to erase was already too deeply rooted in the
ancient world to burn.

PART 7
LEGACY OF ANCIENT PERSIA

Chapter 17
The Persian Model of Empire

When Alexander the Great swept through the Persian heartland in 330 BCE and burned Persepolis to the ground, many observers might have concluded that the Achaemenid way of ruling the world had died with it. They would have been wrong. The administrative genius of the Persian Empire - its division of vast territories into manageable provinces, its tolerance of local customs, its sophisticated use of roads and communication networks - proved far more durable than any palace or dynasty. Empires rose and fell across the Iranian plateau for the next thousand years, and nearly every one of them borrowed, consciously or not, from the Persian blueprint.

From the Parthians, who reclaimed Iran from the successors of Alexander, to the Sassanids, who built one of antiquity's most sophisticated states, to the early Islamic caliphates that absorbed and adapted what came before them - the Persian model of empire echoed across centuries. Understanding that echo helps explain not just how these states were organized, but why certain ideas about kingship, administration, and cultural identity proved so remarkably resilient.

The Achaemenid Blueprint

Before examining what was inherited, it helps to understand what was being passed down.

At its height, the Achaemenid Persian Empire stretched from the Aegean coast of Anatolia to the Indus Valley - a territory so vast that no single ruler could govern it through personal presence alone. The solution the Persians developed was the satrapy: a regional administrative unit governed by a satrap, or provincial governor, who held considerable local authority while remaining accountable to the king. Each satrap collected taxes, maintained order, and administered justice within their territory, but the king's inspectors - sometimes called "the eyes and ears of the king" - traveled the empire to ensure loyalty and compliance.

This system was not merely practical. It was philosophically distinctive. Rather than demanding cultural uniformity from conquered peoples, the Achaemenids generally permitted local languages, religions, and customs to continue. Cyrus the Great famously allowed the Jews exiled in Babylon to return to their homeland. Local elites were often retained in administrative roles. The empire projected power not primarily through cultural erasure but through integration - drawing conquered peoples into a functioning system rather than simply crushing them beneath it.

That combination of centralized oversight and local flexibility became the template that successive Iranian empires would return to, again and again.

The Parthians: Heirs by Necessity

When the Parthians - known in Persian tradition as the Ashkani - wrested control of the Iranian plateau from the Seleucid successors of Alexander during the third and second centuries BCE, they inherited a world shaped by both Persian and Hellenistic influences. Their challenge was to govern an enormous, diverse territory with a relatively lean administrative apparatus.

Their solution drew heavily on what had come before. The Parthian Empire organized its territories into regional units that functioned much like the old Achaemenid satrapies - semi-autonomous zones governed by local dynasts and nobles who owed loyalty to the Arsacid royal house. This was not a carbon copy of the Persian model, but it carried the same essential logic: a large empire could be held together through a network of loyal regional powers, each managing their own affairs within limits set from the center.

The Parthians also inherited the Persian appreciation for royal ceremony and symbolic authority. Their kings presented themselves as heirs to a long Iranian tradition of legitimate kingship - a tradition that stretched back, in the cultural memory of the region, to the great Achaemenid rulers. In a world where political legitimacy was inseparable from historical and religious narrative, claiming continuity with Cyrus and Darius carried real weight. This was not mere vanity. It was statecraft.

Reconstructions from available historical sources reveal a Parthian society in which old Persian frameworks had been adapted rather than abandoned. Local elites retained influence. Regional customs persisted. The empire functioned less as a monolithic state than as a confederation of relationships, bound together by shared interest and the prestige of the Arsacid crown.

The Sassanids: Systematizing the Inheritance

If the Parthians adapted the Persian model loosely, the Sassanids refined it into something more deliberate and more powerful.

Rising to power in the third century CE, the Sassanid dynasty explicitly positioned itself as the restorer of authentic Persian greatness. Where the Parthians had been relatively decentralized, the Sassanids moved toward a more structured imperial administration - one that bore clear marks of Achaemenid influence even as it evolved in new directions. Provincial governance remained essential to the system, but the Sassanid state worked to bring regional power more firmly under royal control, reducing the autonomy of the great noble houses that had sometimes made Parthian rule feel more like a loose alliance than a unified empire.

The Sassanids also formalized the relationship between the state and religion in ways that would prove enormously consequential. Zoroastrianism, the ancient Iranian faith that the Achaemenids had patronized, became under the Sassanids something closer to a state religion - with a priestly hierarchy, the Magi, playing an active role in legitimating royal authority. This fusion of political and religious power was not entirely new to the region, but the Sassanids systematized it in ways that created a template for how empire and faith could reinforce one another.

Their administrative language, Pahlavi, became the medium of government across a vast territory. Their court culture - elaborate, hierarchical, rich in ceremony - set standards that neighboring powers admired and imitated. Byzantine emperors watched the Sassanid court with a mixture of rivalry and envy. When the early Islamic caliphates absorbed the Sassanid territories in the seventh century, they found not a broken state but a sophisticated administrative machine, one that was too useful to discard.

The Islamic Inheritance

The Arab conquests of the seventh century CE transformed the political map of the Middle East and Central Asia with breathtaking speed. Within a generation of the Prophet Muhammad's death in 632 CE, Arab armies had overrun the Sassanid Empire entirely and stripped Byzantium of its richest eastern provinces. But military conquest and administrative governance are different arts, and the early caliphates quickly discovered that running an empire required more than winning battles.

What they found in the former Sassanid territories was a ready-made system. Persian administrators, trained in the traditions of Sassanid governance, became indispensable to the new rulers. The administrative vocabulary of the caliphate absorbed Persian terms and concepts. Provincial governance continued to function along lines that would have been recognizable to a Sassanid official - or, for that matter, to an Achaemenid satrap.

This was not passive absorption. The Abbasid caliphate, which came to power in 750 CE and moved its capital to the newly founded city of Baghdad - built on the Tigris River, deep in the heart of former Sassanid territory - consciously embraced Persian administrative culture. Persian bureaucrats, Persian court ceremonial, and Persian ideas about the nature of kingship all flowed into the Abbasid system. The famous Abbasid court, with its elaborate hierarchy and its cultivation of learning and philosophy, owed more to Sassanid precedent than its Arab founders might always have cared to acknowledge.

The satrapy, in its various adapted forms, had traveled more than a thousand years from Cyrus the Great to the Abbasid caliphs. The names changed. The religions changed. The languages of administration changed. But the underlying logic - that a vast, diverse empire required regional administration, local flexibility, and a strong symbolic center - remained.

Why the Model Endured

Persistence on this scale demands explanation. Why did the Persian administrative model prove so durable across such radically different political and cultural contexts?

Part of the answer is simply practical. The satrapy system worked. It solved a genuine problem - how to govern territory too large for any central authority to manage directly - in a way that balanced control with flexibility. Empires that abandoned it entirely tended to fragment; empires that adopted some version of it tended to cohere.

But there is more to it than efficiency. The Persian model also carried with it a set of ideas about legitimate rule that proved deeply attractive to successor states. The notion that a great king ruled over many peoples, each with their own customs and traditions, while maintaining a universal order - this was a compelling vision of empire, one that offered conquered peoples a place within the system rather than simply beneath it. It was a model of power that could absorb diversity rather than being threatened by it.

Scholars differ on the precise mechanisms by which these administrative traditions were transmitted across centuries and conquests. Direct institutional continuity is sometimes difficult to trace. But the convergence of evidence - in administrative vocabulary, in governance structures, in the symbolic language of kingship - points consistently toward a living inheritance rather than mere coincidence.

Legacy and Long-Term Impact

The Persian model's influence did not stop with the Abbasid caliphate. Administrative traditions that flowed from the Achaemenids through the Parthians and Sassanids into the Islamic world shaped governance structures across a vast arc of history, from the medieval Islamic empires to the Ottoman and Safavid states of the early modern period.

The satrapy, in its many reincarnations, became one of history's most successful administrative ideas - not because it was imposed by force alone, but because it offered a workable answer to one of the oldest problems in political life: how to hold together a world of differences under a single authority.

Quick Summary

- The Achaemenid Persian Empire developed the satrapy system - regional provinces governed by appointed officials - as a solution to governing vast, diverse territories.

- Rather than demanding cultural uniformity, the Persians generally permitted local customs, languages, and religions to continue, making their model of empire unusually flexible.

- The Parthian (Ashkani) Empire adapted this model, organizing its territories into semi-autonomous regional units governed by local dynasts loyal to the Arsacid royal house.

- The Sassanid dynasty refined the inheritance further, moving toward more centralized administration while formalizing the relationship between royal authority and Zoroastrian religious institutions.

- When Arab armies conquered the Sassanid Empire in the seventh century CE, they absorbed Persian administrative personnel, vocabulary, and structures rather than replacing them entirely.

- The Abbasid caliphate, centered at Baghdad from 750 CE, consciously embraced Persian court culture and governance traditions, giving the Persian model new life within an Islamic framework.

- The durability of the Persian model rested on both practical effectiveness and a compelling vision of empire - one that could incorporate diverse peoples rather than simply dominating them.

The Persian model of empire was never a fixed thing. Each civilization that inherited it reshaped it, adapted it, and made it their own. But across more than a millennium - from the court of Cyrus the Great to the halls of the Abbasid caliphs - something essential persisted: the idea that great power and cultural tolerance were not opposites, but partners. That idea, forged on the Iranian plateau in the sixth century BCE, would continue to echo long after the last Sassanid king had fallen and the last Parthian coin had been buried in the earth.

Chapter 18
Persia's Enduring Cultural Impact

When Cyrus the Great rode into Babylon in 539 BCE, he did something no conqueror before him had thought to do: he let the people keep their gods.

He freed enslaved populations, restored temples, and declared that the peoples under his rule had the right to live according to their own customs. This wasn't weakness. It was a philosophy - one rooted in a vision of human dignity that the ancient world had rarely seen and that the modern world still struggles to fully achieve. That philosophy didn't die when Alexander the Great toppled the Achaemenid throne in 330 BCE. It survived, adapted, and quietly shaped the civilizations that came after.

Why does Persia still matter? The answer reaches into the foundations of Western and Eastern religion, into the architecture of modern governance, and into the very idea that a diverse empire of many peoples can be held together not by fear alone, but by something approaching shared values. Persia's legacy is not a relic. It is a living inheritance.

A Faith That Shaped an Empire

To understand Persia's cultural legacy, you have to begin with Zoroaster - the prophet known in his own language as Zarathustra - and the religion he founded that would become the spiritual backbone of the Achaemenid world.

Zoroastrianism is one of the oldest monotheistic religions in human history. At its core, it teaches a cosmic struggle between truth and falsehood, light and darkness, good and evil. Ahura Mazda, the supreme deity, represents wisdom and righteousness. Against him stands Angra Mainyu, the destructive spirit. Every human being, in

Zoroastrian thought, participates in this struggle through their choices - through their words, their thoughts, and their deeds.

This was not merely theology. It was a moral framework with direct political consequences.

When the Achaemenid kings - Cyrus, Darius, Xerxes, and their successors - ruled over an empire stretching from Egypt to the borders of India, they governed under the assumption that truth and justice were cosmic obligations, not political conveniences. Royal inscriptions from Darius I repeatedly invoke Ahura Mazda and frame the king's duty as the protection of truth against the lie. Governance, in this worldview, was a sacred responsibility.

That idea - that power carries moral weight, that rulers are accountable to something higher than themselves - would echo through centuries of political thought long after the last Achaemenid king was gone.

The Empire That Held Together by Letting Go

What made the Achaemenid Empire remarkable was not simply its size, though it was the largest empire the world had yet seen. What made it remarkable was its method.

Cyrus the Great, who founded the empire around 550 BCE, built his dominion on a principle that ran against the grain of ancient conquest: respect for the cultures, religions, and customs of subject peoples. Where Assyrian kings had deported populations and smashed temples as instruments of control, Cyrus restored them. He allowed the Jewish exiles in Babylon to return to their homeland and rebuild their temple - an act recorded in the Hebrew Bible and remembered to this day.

This was not naive generosity. It was sophisticated statecraft. By allowing conquered peoples to maintain their identities, Cyrus reduced the friction of empire. He transformed potential rebels into stakeholders. The Achaemenid system of satrapies - regional governors who administered local affairs under imperial oversight - was similarly pragmatic. Local languages, legal customs, and religious practices were preserved within a framework of Persian authority.

The result was something genuinely new in the ancient world: a multiethnic, multilingual, multireligious empire that functioned not as a machine of cultural erasure but as a kind of federation of identities held together by shared governance and mutual obligation.

Whether this model was always perfectly realized is another matter - empires are never as clean as their ideals. But the aspiration itself was transformative, and its influence on later imperial models, from the Hellenistic kingdoms that followed Alexander to the Roman Empire's own experiments in provincial governance, was substantial.

What Persia Gave to Greece - and Through Greece, to Us

Here is one of history's great ironies: the civilization that Greece spent decades fighting became one of its most important teachers.

Persian culture flowed into the Greek world through trade, diplomacy, warfare, and the movement of people across borders. Artistic motifs, administrative techniques, and philosophical ideas all left marks on Greek civilization. When Alexander conquered the Achaemenid Empire in 330 BCE, his armies didn't simply destroy what they found - they absorbed it. Alexander himself adopted Persian court customs, Persian dress, and Persian administrative structures. His successors, the Hellenistic kings, ruled over hybrid cultures in which Persian and Greek traditions intertwined.

Zoroastrian ideas about cosmic dualism - the struggle between good and evil, light and darkness - filtered into the religious thought of the ancient Mediterranean world. Scholars have traced threads of Zoroastrian influence into Jewish apocalyptic literature, early Christian theology, and Gnostic philosophy. The concept of a final judgment, of heaven and hell as distinct destinations for the righteous and the wicked, of a savior figure who would appear at the end of time - all of these ideas have parallels in Zoroastrian thought that predate their appearance in Western religious traditions.

None of this means Zoroastrianism directly caused these developments. Religious ideas travel in complex, contested ways, and historians rightly debate the precise nature of these influences. But the presence of Persian thought at the crossroads of the ancient world - at the moment when Judaism, early Christianity, and Greek philosophy were all taking shape - was not coincidental. Persia was there, and its ideas were in the air.

Identity, Legacy, and the Long Memory of Civilization

Empires end. Cultures don't - at least not quickly.

When Alexander dismantled the Achaemenid Empire, he burned Persepolis, the great ceremonial capital that Darius I had built as a monument to Persian power and identity. It was a symbolic act of conquest. But the culture Persepolis represented proved far more durable than its stones.

Persian language, literature, and artistic traditions survived the Macedonian conquest, the subsequent Seleucid rule, and the rise of the Parthian and Sasanian empires that followed. Persian became the literary and administrative language of vast stretches of the Islamic world after the Arab conquests of the seventh century CE - a remarkable persistence for a culture that had supposedly been conquered and absorbed. The great Persian poets, the traditions of Persian miniature painting, the architectural legacy of Persian garden design - all of these continued to shape the cultures of Central Asia, the Indian subcontinent, and the Middle East long after the last Achaemenid king had been dead for centuries.

This is what genuine cultural vitality looks like. Not the survival of a single dynasty or a single political structure, but the persistence of a way of seeing the world - a set of values, aesthetic sensibilities, and philosophical commitments that prove useful and beautiful enough that people keep returning to them.

Why This Still Matters

It would be easy to treat Persia as a chapter in a textbook - important once, now safely historical. That would be a mistake.

The questions that Achaemenid Persia grappled with are the same questions that every complex, diverse society faces today. How do you govern people who do not share a single language, religion, or cultural tradition? What obligations does power carry? Can an empire - or a nation - hold together through respect rather than coercion alone?

Cyrus the Great didn't answer these questions perfectly. No ruler does. But the fact that he asked them at all, and that his answers were sophisticated enough to build the largest empire the ancient world had yet seen, tells us something important about the range of human political imagination.

Zoroastrianism, meanwhile, remains a living religion practiced by communities in Iran, India, and around the world. Its emphasis on truth, justice, and the moral responsibility of the individual connects ancient Persian thought to concerns that feel urgently contemporary. The Zoroastrian insistence that good and evil are not abstract forces but choices made by real people in real moments carries a weight that no amount of historical distance diminishes.

And the model of cultural pluralism that Cyrus embodied - however imperfectly - has never stopped being relevant. Every generation rediscovers the difficulty of building a society that honors difference without dissolving into chaos, that maintains order without crushing identity. Persia tried. Its successes and failures alike are instructive.

Key Takeaways

- Cyrus the Great founded the Achaemenid Empire around 550 BCE and established a model of governance based on respect for the cultures, religions, and customs of conquered peoples.

- Zoroastrianism, one of the world's oldest monotheistic religions, provided the moral and philosophical framework for Achaemenid rule, emphasizing truth, justice, and individual moral responsibility.

- The Achaemenid system of satrapies allowed local governance within a broader imperial structure, making the empire more stable and more culturally diverse than most of its predecessors.

- Persian cultural influence flowed into Greek civilization, and through the Hellenistic world, into the religious and philosophical traditions of Judaism, early Christianity, and Gnostic thought.

- Alexander's conquest in 330 BCE ended the Achaemenid dynasty but did not erase Persian culture, which persisted through subsequent empires and continued to shape Central Asia, the Middle East, and the Indian subcontinent.

- Persian language and literary traditions became foundational to Islamic civilization after the seventh-century Arab conquests, demonstrating the remarkable durability of Persian cultural identity.

- Zoroastrianism remains a living religion today, and its core ideas about cosmic justice, moral choice, and the struggle between good and evil continue to resonate across cultures and centuries.

Civilizations are not simply political structures that rise and fall. They are ways of understanding the world - and the most powerful ones leave behind not just ruins but ideas. Persia gave the ancient world a vision of empire built on something more than force, a religion built on something more than ritual, and a model of human dignity that proved stubborn enough to outlast conquest, assimilation, and the long erosion of time. Across the centuries that followed, every culture that grappled with questions of justice, identity, and the right use of power was, in some measure, still answering questions that Persia first asked.

You did it.

You have just traveled across three thousand years of history - from the earliest stirrings of Persian identity on the Iranian plateau to the moment Alexander's torches lit the halls of Persepolis. You have walked the Royal Road, sat in the shadow of the Apadana, and seen one of history's greatest civilizations not through the eyes of its enemies, but on its own terms.

That is no small thing. Most people never look past the Greek narrative. You did.

The Persian Empire was not a backdrop to someone else's story. It was a world unto itself - a world of extraordinary administration, breathtaking art, remarkable tolerance, and genuine human complexity. The workers who built Persepolis were paid wages. The peoples of twenty satrapies kept their languages, their gods, and their customs. Cyrus wept at the tomb of a fallen enemy king. These are not the details of a tyranny. They are the details of a civilization that deserved - and still deserves - to be understood.

Carrying that understanding forward is its own reward. But there is one small thing you can do that would mean a great deal.

If this book gave you something - a new perspective, a moment of genuine surprise, a sense that history is richer and stranger than you were taught - please consider leaving a review. It does not need to be long. A sentence or two is more than enough. Reviews are how independent history books find their readers, and every single one makes a difference. Your words could be the reason someone else picks this book up, and begins their own journey into ancient Persia.

Thank you for reading. Thank you for your curiosity. And thank you, above all, for giving the Persians a fair hearing.